GREYSTONE'S
Creative Hands

EDITOR

Beverley Hilton

GREYSTONE PRESS/NEW YORK · TORONTO · LONDON

Volume 5

© Fratelli Fabri Editore, Milan 1966, 1967
Marshall Cavendish Limited 1970, 1971, 1972, 1973, 1975
Manufactured in the United States of America
Library of Congress Catalog Card No. 75-8338

Much of the material contained herein has previously been published in separate parts under the title Golden Hands.

Contents

Pattern Library

Appliqué Dress

This enchanting dress with its prettily scalloped cape sleeves and attractive appliquéd bodice panel was designed by Adele Cooper, a fashion student at a London art college. The dress is made in cream rayon crepe, with satin and crepe appliqué in dark green, pale green, pink, blue and cream, worked by machine with a zigzag stitch. The appliqué panel shows two birds perched at the edge of a lake surrounded by trees, with soft pink clouds above. The appliqué pattern is decorated by hand with satin stitch and French knots.

Striped for effect

Stripes of one or more colors are easy to work and instructions for achieving two different effects are given in this chapter. Wide or narrow stripes in stockinette stitch can give an unbroken line of new color on the background fabric; on the reverse or purl side, the line of color is broken by the loops of the previous row. It is this second technique which has been used as part of the sweater pattern given on the next page. If you try it, you'll not only see how simple stripes are, but add to your wardrobe at the same time!

Ribbed stripes

In the illustration of the pink, green and yellow striped knitted pattern, the broken line of colors on the purl stitches can be seen easily and it is also possible to see how the uneven effect is heightened by the use of ribbing.

Cast on a number of stitches divisible by 10, plus 5, using green.

1st row. Using green P5, *K1, ytf, sl 1P, ytb, K1, ytf, sl 1P, ytb, K1, P5, rep from * to end.

2nd row. Using green K1, ytf, sl 1P, ytb, K1, ytf, sl 1P, ytb, K1, *P5, K1, ytf, sl 1P, ytb, K1, ytf, sl 1P, ytb, K1, rep from * to end.

Rep 1st and 2nd rows twice.

Rep 1st and 2nd rows 4 times, using yellow.

Rep 1st and 2nd rows once, using green.

Rep 1st and 2nd rows 3 times, using pink.

Rep 1st and 2nd rows once, using green.

Rep 1st and 2nd rows 3 times, using pink.

Rep 1st and 2nd rows once, using green.

Rep 1st and 2nd rows 4 times, using yellow.

These 40 rows form the pattern.

Chevron stripes

A zigzag striped effect can be made by the clever use of stitch changes added to color changes. The illustration shows simple stripes of four rows of each color, and the chevron shaping is formed by the vertical lines of increased and decreased stitches.

Cast on a number of stitches divisible by 14, using white.

1st row. Using white, *K1, inc by knitting into the loop below the next stitch on the left-hand needle and then K the stitch immediately above, K4, sl 1P, K2 tog, psso, K4, inc as before, rep from * to end.

2nd row. Using white, P.

3rd row. Using white, as 1st.

4th row. Using white, as 2nd.

Continue working four rows in this manner in tones of pink and red (the illustration shows four tones), then four rows in white followed by four rows of tones of beige and brown (four tones are illustrated).

442

▲ *Ribbed striped pattern*   ▼ *Chevron striped pattern*

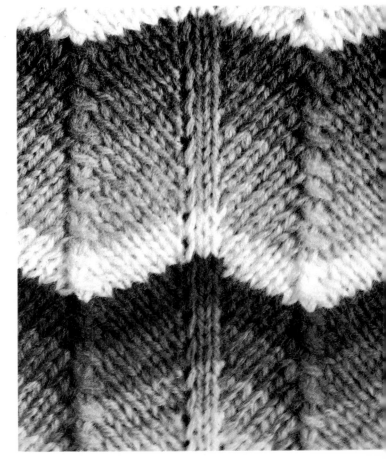

Make yourself a striped jersey

Sizes

Directions are for 32in bust. The figures in brackets [] refer to the 34, 36 and 38in sizes respectively.
Length down center back, 21½in.
Sleeve seam, 6in.

Gauge

6¼sts to 1in over st st worked on No.4 needles. (Measure gauge over 25sts for accuracy.)

Materials

Sports Yarn (2oz skeins)
3 skeins of main color A
1 skein of 1st contrast B
1 skein of 2nd contrast C
One pair No.3 needles (or Canadian No.10)
One pair No.4 needles (or Canadian No.9)

Back and Front (alike)

Using No.3 needles and A, cast on 96[102:108:114] sts.
1st row *K1, P1, rep from * to end.
Rep 1st row 7 times more.
Change to No.4 needles and reversed st st, beg with a P row.
Inc one st at each end of 7th and then every 16th row until there are 108[114:120:126] sts; at the same time work in stripes as follows:
4 rows A
4 rows B
6 rows C
10 rows B
4 rows C
10 rows B
10 rows A
4 rows C
10 rows A
8 rows B
8 rows C
8 rows B

Shape armholes

1st row Using A, bind off 3[4:5:6], P to end.
2nd row Using A, bind off 3[4:5:6], K to end.
3rd row Using A, P3, sl 1P, P1, psso, P to last 5sts, P2 tog, P3.

4th row Using A, K.
Rep last 2 rows once more.
Continue dec in this way until 74[78:82:86] sts rem.
Work in stripes as follows:
6 rows C
10 rows B
4 rows C
8 rows B
10 rows A
2 rows C
4 rows A
Continue using A only.

Shape neck

1st row P31[32:33:34], bind off 12[14:16:18], P31 [32:33:34].
Complete this shoulder first.
K 1 row.
3rd row Bind off 8sts, P to end.
K 1 row. Bind off.
With WS of work facing, attach yarn to rem sts and K to end. P 1 row.
Next row Bind off 8sts, K to end.
P 1 row. Bind off.

Sleeves (make two)

Using No.3 needles and A, cast on 60[64:68:72] sts.
Work 8 rows K1, P1 rib.
Change to No.4 needles.
Work in reversed st st throughout, beg with a P row and inc one st at each end of 9th and every 12th row until there are 66[68:72:74] sts.
Continue without shaping until work measures 6in from beg, ending with a K row.

Shape cap

1st row Bind off 3[4:5:6] sts, P to end.
2nd row Bind off 3[4:5:6] sts, K to end.
Rep 3rd and 4th rows as for back armhole decreasing until 32[32:34:34] sts rem.
Work 50[52:52:54] rows without shaping. Bind off.

Neckband

Press all pieces under a damp cloth with a warm iron.
Sew sleeves from underarm to shoulder edge.
Sew both front seams along straight bound-off edge; also left back seam.

Reversed stockinette stitched raglan-sleeved sweater in three colors

Using No.3 needles, with RS facing and A, pick up and K 28[30:32:34] sts along back edge, 32[32:34:34] sts from left sleeve cap, rep along front edge and other sleeve cap. 120[124:132:136] sts.
1st row *(K1, P1) 16 [16:17:17] times to corner, (K1,P1) 14[15:16:17] times to corner, rep from * once.
2nd row *K2 tog, rib 24[26:28:30], (K2 tog) twice, rib 28[28:30:30], K2 tog, rep from * once.
3rd and every alt row Rib.
4th row *K2 tog, rib 22[24:26:28], (K2 tog) twice, rib 26[26:28:28], K2 tog, rep from * once.
6th row *K2 tog, rib 20[22:24:26], (K2 tog) twice, rib 24[24:26:26], K2 tog,

rep from * once.
8th row *Inc in next st, rib 20 [22:24:26], (inc in next st) twice, rib 24[24:26:26], inc in next st, rep from * once.
10th row *Inc in next st, rib 22[24:26:28], (inc in next st) twice, rib 26[26:28:28], inc in next st, rep from * once.
12th row *Inc in next st, rib 24[26:28:30], (inc in next st) twice, rib 28[28:30:30], inc in next st, rep from * once.
Bind off loosely in rib.

Finishing

Sew right back shoulder seam along bound-off edge. Press seams. Sew sleeve and side seams. Fold neck, sleeve and lower edge ribbing in half and sl st to WS.

443

Stripes are child's play

Striped sweaters for a boy or a girl are child's play to knit in simple stockinette stitch, and the round neckline and the easy-fitting raglan sleeves make them ideal garments for indoor and outdoor play. Although stripes in blending or contrasting colors give a sporty look, the pattern can also be worked in a single color to make a simple classic sweater. The directions cover a wide size range.

Sizes

Directions are for 24in chest. The figures in brackets [] refer to the 26, 28, 30 and 32in chest sizes respectively. Side seam, $7\frac{1}{2}[9:10:11:12\frac{1}{2}]$in. Sleeve seam, $9[10\frac{1}{2}:12\frac{1}{4}:13\frac{1}{2}:15]$in.

Gauge
6sts and 8 rows to 1in over stockinette stitch worked on No.5 needles.

Materials

Sports Yarn (2oz skeins) 2[3:3:3:3] skeins in main color A
2 skeins in contrast B
For a plain pullover, 4[5:5:5:5] skeins in one color.
One pair No.3 needles (or Canadian No.10)
One pair No.5 needles (or Canadian No.8)
Stitch holder

Back

Using No.3 needles and A, cast on 80[86:92:98:104]sts. Work 14[16:18:18:18] rows K1, P1 rib.

Change to No.5 needles and st st.
Beg with a K row, work in stripes as follows:
1st-6th rows Using A.
7th-10th rows Using B.
11th-12th rows Using A.
13th-14th rows Using B.
15th-16th rows Using A.
17th-18th rows Using B.
19th-20th rows Using A.
21st-24th rows Using B.
These 24 rows form the patt and are rep throughout.
Work 24[34:40:48:60] more rows of patt, ending with a 24th [10th:16th:24th:12th] patt row.

Work raglan shaping

Bind off 1[1:2:2:3] sts at beg of next 2 rows.
3rd row K2, sl 1P, K1, psso, K to last 4sts, K2 tog, K2.
4th row P.
Keeping striped patt correct, rep last 2 rows until 30[32:34:36:38]sts rem, ending with a P row.
Slip rem sts on holder.

Front

Work as for back until 42[44:46:48:50] sts rem on raglan shaping, ending with a P row.

Shape neck

1st row K2, K2 tog tbl, K10, turn. Work right shoulder on these sts.
** Keeping raglan shaping correct as before, dec one st at neck edge on next 6 rows. Continue raglan shaping until 3sts rem, ending with WS row.**
Next row K1, K2 tog.
Last row P2 tog. Draw yarn through and fasten off.

With RS facing, slip center 14[16:18:20:22] sts onto holder. Attach yarn to rem sts and work to end of row.
Work from ** to ** as for right shoulder.
Next row K2 tog, K1.
Last row P2 tog. Draw yarn through and fasten off.

Sleeves

Using No.3 needles and A, cast on 38[40:42:44:46] sts. Work 14[18:18:20:20] rows K1, P1 rib, inc one st at each end of last row.
Change to No.5 needles and st st. Continue working in striped patt as for back, beg with 15th [15th:7th:7th:7th] patt row and inc one st at each end of 3rd and then every 6th [6th:8th:8th:8th] row until there are 56[60:64:68:72] sts.
Work without shaping until next 24th [10th:16th:24th:12th] patt row has been completed.

Shape raglan

Bind off 1[1:2:2:3] sts at beg of next 2 rows.
3rd row K2, sl 1P, K1, psso, K to last 4sts, K2 tog, K2.
4th row P.
Rep last 2 rows until 8sts rem, ending with a P row.
Slip rem sts on holder.

Neckband

Using No.3 needles and A, with RS facing, K across 30[32:34:36:38] sts from back neck, K across 8sts from left sleeve cap, pick up and K 12sts down neck, K across 14[16:18:20:22] sts from center front, pick up and K 12sts up neck and K across 8sts from right sleeve cap. 84[88:92:96:100] sts.
Work 16[16:18:18:18] rows K1, P1 rib. Bind off in rib.

Finishing

DO NOT PRESS.
Sew raglan, side and sleeve seams. Fold neckband in half to WS and sl st.

Warm enough to wear outdoors ▶

The fine edge on knits

One of the great things about crochet is the many different edge variations you can make with it. You don't need to limit yourself to using these edgings as trimmings for household linen or crochet garments. A little experimenting will show you that they can look just as attractive as borders on knitted garments, too. Try trimming a plain reversed stockinette stitch sweater with single crochet in a contrasting color to make a simple neckline more interesting. This chapter gives you four edgings to choose from.

How to work a neat edge

The first row of crochet must be worked evenly onto the knitted edge for a neat and attractive crochet design. If the stitches of this first row are worked unevenly, the finished appearance will be completely spoiled.

The simplest of all edgings is formed by working two or more rows of single crochet along the garment edge. The illustration shows a plain, raglan-sleeved sweater finished in this way. Leave the front left raglan seam open for approximately 5 inches and, with the right side of the work facing, pick up stitches evenly along the front raglan edge, right around the neck and down the sleeve edge of the raglan. Work in single crochet and make two single crochets in each stitch at the top corners of the raglan seam opening. Turn and work three more rows of single crochet around the edges. Work two single crochet into the top of the raglan seam

Detail of sweater neck with Velcro fastening

Raglan sweater showing crochet neck edging

opening for neat corners. Fasten off and darn in ends. Overlap the front edge over the sleeve edge and sew down the bottom of the raglan seam opening. Use a fastening such as Velcro, or just snaps to close the opening.

Here we give you four more edges which can be worked just as quickly and easily. Use them as borders on the front of a plain cardigan or around the cuffs and neck of a basic sweater to give a couture finish to your favorite pattern.

Crab stitch edging

This is the simplest of all the variations of single crochet and can be worked backward and forward along an edge in rows, or continuously around a circular opening such as a cuff.

1st row. Work along edge using single crochet. If working a circular edge, join with a slip stitch to the first stitch.

2nd row. If the work is circular, work back along the round already made, working one single crochet in each single crochet and working from left to right instead of the normal right to left. If you are working in rows, then do not turn the work; simply make one single crochet in each single crochet already made. Fasten off.

Reversed crab stitch edging

1st row. Work along edge using single crochet. Turn.

2nd row. Ch2, skip first single crochet, *1sc into next sc, rep from * to end. Do not turn.

3rd row. Into each sc of previous row work 1sc, working from left to right. Fasten off.

Twisted stitch edging

1st row. Work along edge using single crochet. Turn.

2nd row. *Insert hook into first sc, yoh and draw a loop through loosely, turn the hook on itself in order to twist the stitches, yoh and draw through all loops, rep from * to end. Fasten off.

Cluster stitch edging

1st row. Work along edge using single crochet. Break yarn.

The 2nd row is worked in the same direction as the 1st.

2nd row. Join yarn with ss to first sc, ch2, *1sc into next sc, (yoh, insert hook into ch to right of sc just worked and draw through one loose st) times into same stitch, yoh and draw through all loops, ch1, skip 1sc, rep from * to end. Fasten off.

▲ *Crab stitch edging*　　　　　▼ *Reverse crab stitch edging*

▲ *Twisted stitch edging*　　　　　▼ *Cluster stitch edging*

Embroidery 23

Smocking for little angels

Children of all ages look delightful in smocked clothes —babies in angel tops, nine year-olds in frilled blouses and fashion-conscious growing girls in smocked party dresses. This chapter gives instructions for making a smocked angel top from a graph pattern to fit babies from birth to six months old. The neckline and cuffs are smocked with two of the three stitches illustrated, trellis stitch and outline stitch. Smocking stitches vary in their degree of fabric control. Some have tight control, others medium or loose control. It is important when planning smocking to note the control of the stitches selected. This angel top, for instance, uses a loose control stitch—trellis stitch —on the bottom edge of the smocking, so that the fabric flares.

Outline stitch. Similar to ordinary outline stitch in embroidery (see diagram), each stitch picks up one tube of the fabric. A firm control stitch, two rows worked closely together at the top or base of smocking will hold gathers firmly in place. It is not advisable to use this stitch at the base of smocking where a loose flare is required (such as an angel top).

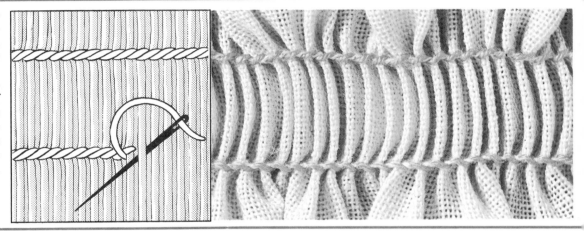

Honeycomb stitch. This is a medium control stitch and is worked from left to right. Bring the needle up at the top of the first tube and make a backstitch picking up the next tube on the right. Take a second backstitch, slipping the needle through the tube and bring it to the right side, ready to make the next double backstitch.

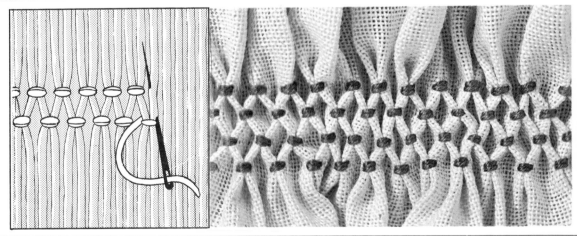

Trellis stitch. Worked in zigzag lines, this stitch is shown on the illustrated angel top and is on the cuffs. It is a loose control stitch and could be used for the last row of smocking where a flare is required.

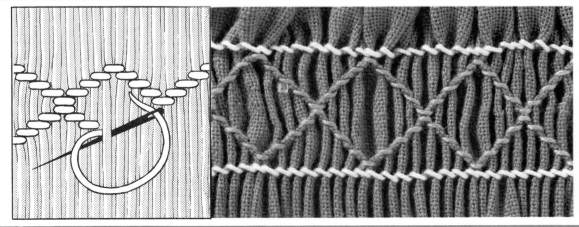

Making a smocked angel top

You will need

- ☐ 2½yds of washable fabric such as Dacron and cotton, cotton, or wool and cotton mixtures.
- ☐ Length of gathering dots transfer
- ☐ Pearl cotton embroidery thread

Preparing for smocking

Make a paper pattern from the angel top graph and pin this to the fabric. Cut out the pieces and iron the required length and depth of gathering dots transfer to the wrong side of the fabric. Gather on the wrong side (Embroidery chapter 22, page 428) and complete the smocking on each part of the angel top before sewing the garment together.

Making the top

Join sleeves to dress, trimming seams to ¼ inch depth. Overcast or bind the seams with bias binding or binding bias cut from the same fabric. Cut a neckband and two cuffs on the cross of the fabric to fit the child's neck and wrists. The neckband and cuffs should always be attached to the garment with hand sewing because if machine stitching is used, the pleats or "tubes" of smocked fabric would be pushed flat

Make two rows of gathering ¼ inch above the top line of smocking stitches. The rows of gathering stitches should be placed exactly in line, one stitch above the other, and evenly through each "tube" of fabric. Draw up the gathering to fit the length of the neckband. Turn under the seam allowance of the neckband along one edge and baste. Place the wrong side of the basted edge ¼ inch above the top line of smocking on the right side of the angel top. Pin and baste. With the right side of the work facing, slip stitch each tube to the neckband evenly. Turn the work to the wrong side. Turn under the seam allowance on the other side of the neckband

and baste to the inside neckline ¼ inch above the top row of smocking. Hem to the backs of the tubes, using small neat stitches. Make sure that the stitches do not show through to the right side of the tubes. Stitch the sleeve and side seams carefully.

Adapting a yoked pattern for smocking

To adapt a nightie or dress pattern so that smocking can be included, choose a pattern with a straight or slightly curved yoke and cut the front three times the width of the actual pattern piece. Attach the yoke to the smocked areas as instructed for applying the crossway edgings to the top.

▲ *Angel top made with a front fastening and ribbon trim*

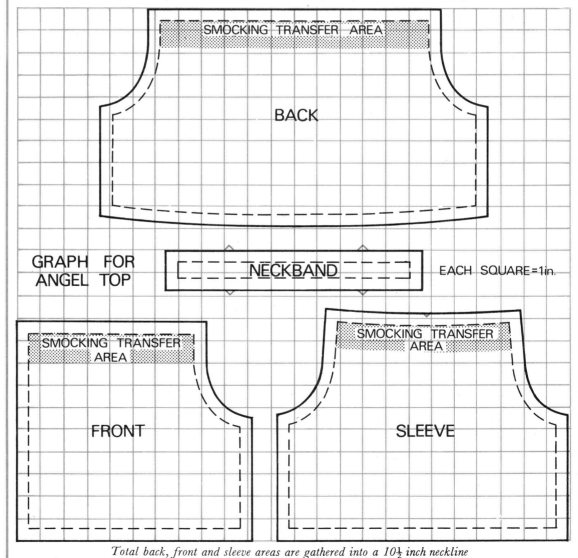

GRAPH FOR ANGEL TOP

SMOCKING TRANSFER AREA

BACK

NECKBAND   EACH SQUARE=1in.

SMOCKING TRANSFER AREA

FRONT

SMOCKING TRANSFER AREA

SLEEVE

Total back, front and sleeve areas are gathered into a 10½ inch neckline

From Libra to Pisces

Is your lucky sign of the zodiac in this chapter? Here are the signs covering the months from September to March—Libra, Scorpio, Sagittarius, Capricorn, Aquarius and Pisces. Work the signs on fine canvas, as suggested in Needlepoint chapter 10, page 310, or enlarge the designs by following the instructions below. Exciting effects can be achieved with coarser canvas, using a greater variety of stitches and yarns.

To enlarge a design you will need

☐ Graph paper ☐ A sharp, soft pencil

You can vary the size of a needlepoint design by working on different weights of canvas—the coarser the canvas, the larger the design. The following instructions can be adapted to enlarge almost any uncomplicated design.

Shade in with pencil four squares of the graph paper for each square on the original chart. Each of the large, penciled squares is then used for either four tent stitches or one square stitch. This enlarged design can now be worked on single-weave canvas, giving scope for a greater variety of stitches such as cushion stitch, rice stitch, double cross-stitch or long-legged cross-stitch, used for either the motif or the background. For instance, try the effect of the motif in rice stitch with the background in cushion stitch or long-legged cross-stitch. Have fun experimenting with different textures—it is surprising how much you can change the look of a design by varying the stitch combinations you use.

The single enlarged design can be used as a central motif on a pillow, bag or stool top. A panel made up of all twelve motifs would look striking, particularly if worked as a sampler, with each motif in a different combination of stitches and threads.

N.B. Sagittarius: To work the bow strings on this motif, stitch the background first and then work two long stitches for the strings. If the article you are decorating needs to withstand hard wear, catch the long threads of the motif with invisible nylon yarn.

▼ *Work your sign of the zodiac as a glamorous belt buckle*

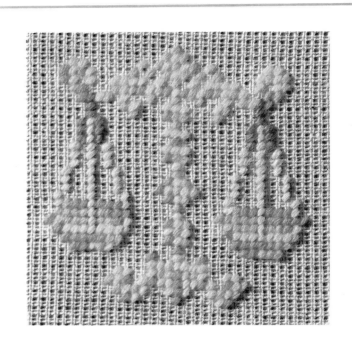

▲ *Libra (Sept 23 to Oct 22)* ▼ *Capricorn (Dec 21 to Jan 19)*

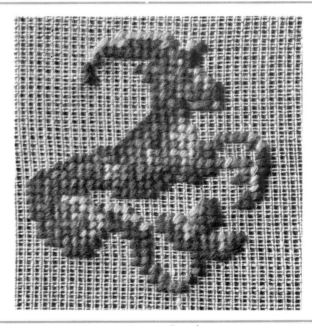

Libra   Scorpio

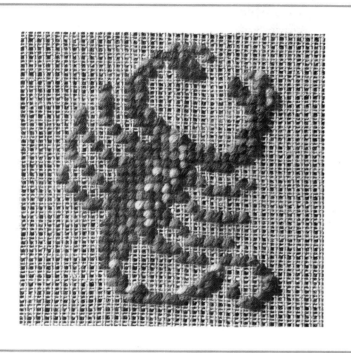

Scorpio (Oct 23 to Nov 22) ▼ *Aquarius (Jan 20 to Feb 18)* ▲ *Sagittarius (Nov 23 to Dec 20)* ▼ *Pisces (Feb 19 to March 20)*

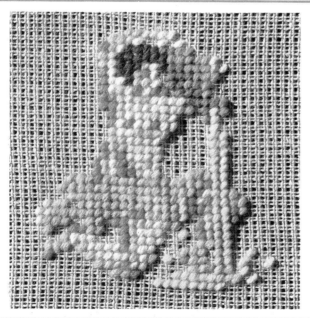

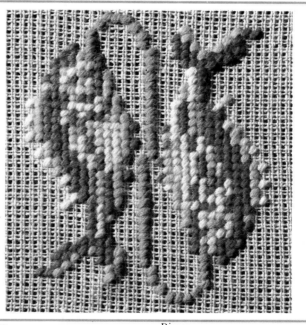

Sagittarius *Capricorn* *Aquarius* *Pisces*

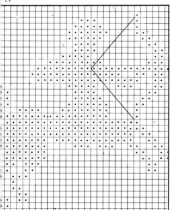

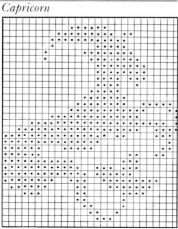

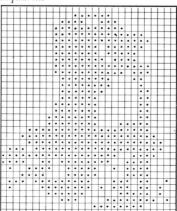

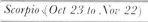

On the fringe of things

Fringing adds a touch of distinction to almost anything and now that you are able to cope with more complicated patterns there are many ways in which you could adapt these fringes. For example, you could make an entire shawl using the beautiful filigree fringe pattern in this chapter. If you feel you need to refresh your memory on the fringing techniques explained in earlier chapters, you can always refer back to Fringing chapter 1, page 26, and Fringing 2, page 52.

The half knot

This knot is simply either stage one or stage two of the flat knot (see Fringing chapter 2, page 52). When half knots are worked in a series, the result is a spiral. The direction in which the work spirals depends entirely on which stage you use—stage one spirals to the right, stage two to the left.

Banister bar fringe

A heavy fringe of thick cotton, three or four inches deep, makes a marvelous finish to the bottom of a window shade. The banister bar fringe would be ideal for this purpose and is worked very

Banister twist formed with half flat knots

simply from flat knots and half knots.

Prepare bunches of four threads and place them on the fabric in sets of two as follows:
* 1 set of two threads, ¼in space, 1 set of two threads, ½in space *
Repeat from * to * across the required width of the fringe.

1st row. Work flat knots on each bunch immediately below the fabric.

2nd row. Divide the threads in each bunch into sets of two and work a row of flat knots, alternated with those of the row above.

3rd row. Repeat as for second row.

4th row. Under each of the flat knots of the previous row, work a series of half knots, approximately six. The banister bar (half knot spiral), however, can be whatever length you wish, although they must all be the same length.

5th row. At the end of each banister bar work a flat knot.

6th-9th rows. Work alternating flat knots.

10th row. Work a banister bar below each flat knot, again to whatever length you require, but longer than those above.

Finish each bar with a tassel (see Fringing chapter 2).

Fringe edge

End each edge of the fringe at half-inch spaces, substituting simple knots for the flat knots which fall at the outer edges.

Filigree fringe

This beautiful fringe, although more complicated than most, is well worth trying and not as difficult to work as it appears. It combines flat knots with chains made of alternating simple knots (see Fringing chapter 1).

Prepare sets of two threads and position them on the material at ¼in intervals.

N.B. The following is the basic pattern and is worked over an even number of sets, but remember that you will need an additional set at each edge. Read through the instructions, following them in the illustration before reading the paragraph on the fringe edge.

1st row. Work a simple knot on each set of threads.

2nd row. Work a row of flat knots using two sets for each knot.

3rd row. Work a row of flat knots, alternating with those in the previous row.

* Work down from the flat knots as follows:

Counting from the left of the illustration, from the fourth, fifth and sixth flat knots, work three rows of alternating flat knots. Next divide each bunch of threads from the first two flat knots (again counting from the left of the illustration) into two sets of two and work simple knots to form four sets of chains.

Unite the four chains in one flat knot, even with the center row of the alternating flat knots just worked, and then continue in four chains until even with the third row of alternating flat knots. From the next flat knot along (the third), work two sets of chains united in one flat knot, even with the flat knot in the four sets of chains, and then continue in chains until even with the rest of the work. Continue in this way along the fringe.

Work two rows of alternating flat knots to link all of the above *

Repeat from * to * twice more, alternating the chains and blocks of flat knots as illustrated.

Finish with tassels and trim the ends.

Fringe edge

Make the left-hand edge at the equivalent of the 14th set of threads (counting from the left of the illustration), working simple knots instead of flat knots at the outer edge of the block and at the end of the last outer chain before the tassel.

Place the right-hand edge at the equivalent of the 3rd set of threads, working simple knots instead of flat knots at the outer edge

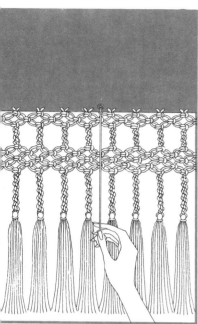

▲ Make a fringe for the edge of a shade. Banister bar fringe formed with flat knots and half knots ▼

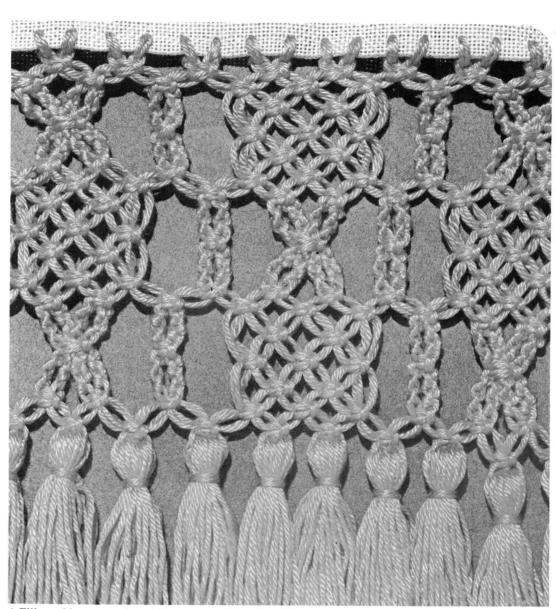

▲ Filigree fringe—very beautiful and not as difficult as it looks   ▼ A flat knot joining two sets of chains

Dress-making 23

Child's flared skirt and vest

Little girls love clothes which coordinate, so this chapter contains patterns and instructions for making a simple flared skirt and matching vest. Both patterns are on a graph, which makes them easy to draft, and both are given in size 10, with instructions for altering the size.

You'll discover as you read on just how versatile the skirt and vest are. You can convert the patterns to other styles and trim the garments in many ways. Trimming ideas are provided as well as patterns and making instructions—and the vest can look just as good on a boy!

The flared skirt and vest in cotton denim, trimmed with rick-rack braid

Girl's flared skirt pattern

This skirt is a simple flare with a center back seam. The pattern is a size 10, which will fit a 25 inch waist, 30 inch hip and is 18 inches long. Each square on the graph equals 1 inch. To make the pattern, copy the back and front sections from the graph onto firm paper in the same way as for the adult flared skirt pattern in Dressmaking chapter 4, page 76. Also follow the same instructions to lengthen or shorten the pattern and alter the size.

Fabric requirements

This skirt takes very little fabric, but as the amount you will need varies so much for each individual child, it is best to work out the yardage on a piece of paper as follows:

When you have made the pattern, take a piece of paper half the width of the skirt fabric (that is, 18 inches for 36 inch wide fabric or 27 inches for 54 inch wide fabric) and lay the pattern on the paper as shown in the diagram, so that the pattern pieces fit economically without overlapping. Add 2 inch hem, 1 inch waist and center back seam allowance and $\frac{3}{4}$ inch for the side seams, just as you would on the fabric.

Pencil in the lines. Then add 3 inches for the waistband and measure the overall length of the paper. This gives you the amount of fabric you will need.

You will also need

☐ Matching thread
☐ 5 to 7 inch skirt zipper (depending on the skirt size)
☐ 1 inch wide belting or other stiffening
☐ 1 inch wide elastic for the waistband
☐ Size No.3 hooks and eyes

Cutting out the fabric

Since the pattern pieces are small, you can use remnants from your own dressmaking or, with clever laying out, you can cut a skirt for yourself and a child from one length. Otherwise, use the paper layout from which you calculated the fabric length, and place the center front along the fold.

Cut out with seam and hem allowances.

Making the skirt

Preparations for making the skirt are the same as those for the adult flared skirt, but here are a few special points to watch.

The hem: The child's flared skirt looks best worn short, and a good deep hem will help the line of the skirt.

The center back seam: There are no darts at the back of the skirt, only the seam. The extra seam allowance helps the skirt to retain a good solid shape.

The waistband: Because there are no darts, a waistband elasticized at the back is used to hold in the fullness which would otherwise be taken into the darts. Full instructions for this waistband follow in this chapter.

If the child has any of the fitting problems mentioned in Dressmaking chapter 13, page 256, make the waistband described in that chapter, ease the fullness into the band at the back for inch, and also add the shoulder straps to the skirt.

Shoulder straps: For a boyish appearance favored by a lot of girls, make the straps about 2 inches wide and add a brace across the front.

Measure the distance between the straps on the waistband and make the brace the same length plus seam allowance.

Attach it to the straps halfway between the shoulder and waistline with small felling stitches. Either embroider the brace with a simple motif or make the brace to cover the width of the straps and attach it with buttons.

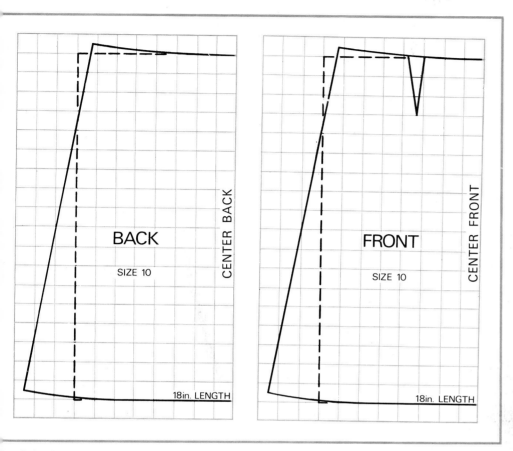

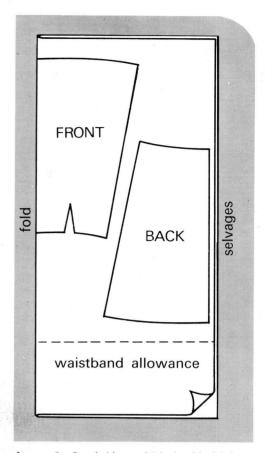

...raph for the child's flared skirt. Seam allowances are not included. Scale: each square equals 1 inch

Layout for flared skirt on 36 inch wide fabric

Making an elasticized waistband

...the skirt is to be worn without straps, ...n elasticized waistband will hold in the ...ack and be the most comfortable answer. ...ubstitute the back half of the waistband ...iffening with 1 inch wide elastic, cut ...inches shorter than the waistband itself. ...ry this around the child's waist first, just ...see how much stretch there is before you ...tch it to the skirt.

...hen attaching an elasticized waistband, ...itch it from the inside to the outside of ...e skirt. This is the reverse of what you ...ve learned so far and there are sound ...asons for this, as the following will ...ow. When you have stitched the stiffen-...g and elastic (stretched to the size of the ...aistband) to the waist seam, you must ...so stitch the elastic to the inside of the ...aistband along the top edges, stretching ...again as it is stitched to equal the waist-...nd in length. Now turn the waistband ...er the stiffening and elastic to the right ...de of the skirt and fold along the seam-...ne as before. Machine stitch along the ...lded edge.

...word of warning when fastening the ...irt: There will be a much greater strain ...the fastening with an elasticized waist-...nd, since the elastic is always held taut, ...use strong hooks and eyes to hold it ...gether. Size No.3 is ideal for this.

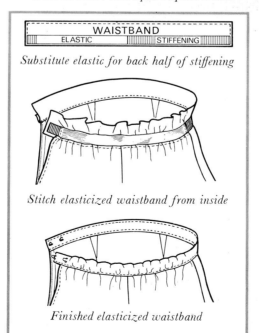

Substitute elastic for back half of stiffening

Stitch elasticized waistband from inside

Finished elasticized waistband

Variations on the flared skirt

There are many ways you can vary this pattern. It can be converted to the four-gore and knife-pleated versions of the adult skirt; or the adult six-gore variation, which comes in Dressmaking chapter 27, page 536, is another possibility.

The dirndl skirt, however, looks better on older children, when the shape of the figure becomes more developed. When using the pattern to make a dirndl for an older child, you must allow more width than the adult pattern. Children's movements are far more exaggerated, and if there is not enough room to allow for this, the skirt will ride up.

You can also vary the skirt with trimmings. There is no limit to the ways in which you can do this. The suggestions given in this chapter are just a starting point—you will be able to add many ideas of your own.

Felling stitch

Felling is a form of hemming one piece of fabric by its edge to another piece. The edge can be folded or left raw. While it is a very strong stitch, it has the added advantage of a neat look.

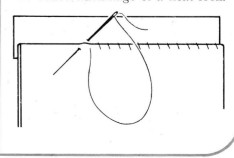

Pretty ideas for trimming the flared skirt

Trimming the flared skirt

If you make the skirt in cotton or linen or any other lightweight fabric, use rows of rick-rack or embroidered cotton braid as a trimming around the hem. A pretty idea for a party skirt is to use rows of guipure daisy chains.

If you make the skirt in wool, work rows of fancy embroidery stitches around the hem. You can also use wool braid, but make sure that this can be cleaned in the same way as the fabric.

When buying braid or other trimming, a useful tip is to buy an extra length to have in reserve when you let the hem down. It is often difficult to remove the hem crease completely after letting a skirt down, and the extra length of braid will hide this unsightly line.

For more practical wear, add different types of pockets as trimmings which you can vary in many attractive ways.

Attaching trims

Rick-rack braid. Leave the hem open before stitching on the braid and use the hemline as a guide. If you stitch the braid on after finishing the hem, you will find it difficult to lengthen the skirt later.

Mark the hemline carefully and measure out the distance between the rows of braid and mark them with basting thread You will find this easier if you have the work lying flat on a table. Lay the braid along the lines you have marked and pin it securely in position. Some braids can be basted down, but others should be pinned so that you are better able to ease the braid onto the fabric as you stitch, and thus avoid large puckers.

The safest way to sew on rick-rack braid is by hand. If you look at the little points closely you will see there is a twist in each one. Sew from point to point with a prick stitch into each twist. On a narrower rick-rack braid use the machine zigzag and work along the center of the braid.

Embroidered braids. Examine the edge of the braid; it should have a good solid finish and look corded.

You should be able to baste on this type of braid quite satisfactorily, so prepare the guide lines as before and baste the braid in place. Stitch it on by hand or machine.

If you use a machine, select a small stitch setting and work close to the edge so that the stitches run along the cording and become part of the braid edge. In this way they will hardly show.

If you are working by hand, use a small prick stitch close to the edge. Never use a felling stitch over the edge of the braid as this looks clumsy. If the braid is thick, use blind stitch to sew it in position.

Heavy lace or guipure. This is one of th most expensive trimmings and requir more time to apply, but it is well worth a the effort.

Guipure lace has a tendency to softe during wear and cleaning, causing th points of the motifs to collapse, but if yo fasten down each point securely, th braid will keep its shape.

Adding pockets

Patch pockets. These are the simple pockets to make.

Cut a square to the size you want, addir $\frac{1}{2}$ inch seam allowance at the side ar lower edges and 1 inch to the upper edg Turn under all the edges and hem th upper one.

If you have trimmed the hem of th skirt with braid, you can use this again trim the pocket before stitching it to t skirt. Topstitch the pocket to the ski close to the edge and fasten off the t corners securely, because they will have stand a lot of strain. If the fabric is thin, is best to underlay these points with a sma piece of fabric before you stitch on t pockets. This strengthens the fabric.

Continental pockets. Cut two squar of fabric the size of the pocket plus sea allowance and a $1\frac{1}{2}$ inch turning for t top opening.

Stitch the pieces together, right sid facing, along the sides and lower edg Turn under the edges around the top ar hem in place. Make two straps 3-4 inch long and $\frac{1}{2}$ inch wide and sew them in each side of the pocket opening. You ca make the straps from the braid you a using if this is strong enough.

Sew a small snap fastener to the insi of the opening to hold it together.

Attach the pocket by stitching the stra between waist seam and waistband.

You can vary the shape and make bucket- or heart-shaped.

Apron pockets. This is an attracti arrangement of a row of pockets across the front of the skirt. Cut a leng of material 6 inches wide and long enou to go right across the front of the ski with a 1 inch seam allowance along t bottom edge and sides and a $\frac{1}{2}$ inch sea allowance along the top edge.

Hem the top edge of the pocket. The before stitching the side seams of the ski stitch on the pocket. Turn in the sea allowance along the bottom edge a stitch it to the skirt. Divide the length in 3 or more equal sections and stitch throu the skirt to make pocket divisions. Stit sides of pockets into skirt side seams.

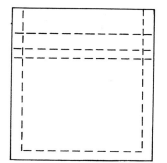

Pattern for patch pocket showing trim

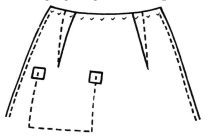

How to underlay pocket corners

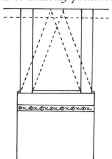

Continental pocket with strap positions

Make a heart-shaped pocket

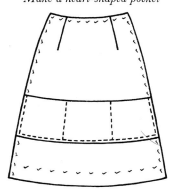

How to attach a row of apron pockets

Blind stitch. This is a more closely worked version of invisible hemming stitch (see Dressmaking 7, page 136).

Prick stitch. This is a version of backstitch (see Dressmaking chapter 2, page 34) worked over a single grain of fabric and forming a tiny surface stitch.

Sewing on snap fasteners. First sew on the ball section of the snap to the upper section of the opening. Press against the lower section of the opening, leaving a tiny mark to show the position for the socket section. Oversew into one hole two or three times, passing the needle under the snap to the next hole until the snap fastener has been firmly attached.

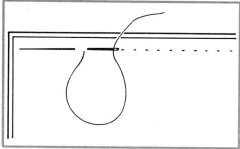
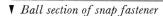

▲ *Blind stitch*   ▼ *Prick stitch*

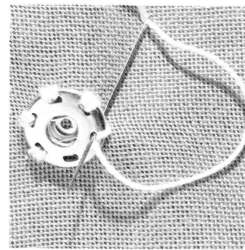

▼ *Ball section of snap fastener*   ▼ *Socket section of snap fastener*

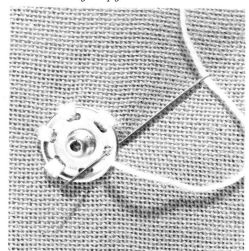

▼ *Ball section of snap fastener goes on front part of opening and socket section goes on back*

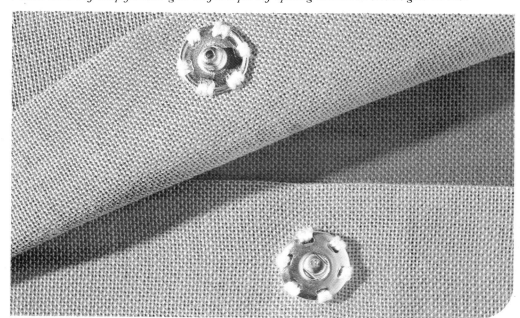

1. Bolero with simple embroidered motifs
2. The basic vest fastened with link buttons
3. Boy's version of the basic vest with pockets and strip fringing
4. Square-fronted bolero with frog fastenings
5. Round-fronted version trimmed with ball fringe

The child's vest

For an attractive outfit for a little girl, coordinate the flared skirt with a smart matching vest. The basic pattern is for a fully lined, edge-to-edge vest with squared or rounded lower front edges. Make it either waist length for a bolero look, or hip length, and let your child choose the trimming.

The pattern

The pattern on the graph is a size 10 and will fit a 28 to 30 inch chest. Instructions for making it larger or smaller are given here. Each square on the graph represents a 1 inch square.

The pattern should be drawn onto graph paper. If you find this difficult to obtain use any firm paper and draw it up into 1 inch squares yourself, but do be very careful to draw it up accurately or the pattern will be distorted.

Cut two pieces of paper 10 inches by 2 inches, one for the back and the other for the front. Following the outline of the version you have chosen, draw the pattern pieces to scale from the graph and also copy all the pattern details.

To adjust the pattern size

The pattern pieces are adjusted along the broken horizontal and vertical lines.

Measure the child's chest, the length from the center of the shoulder to the waist, and from the waist to the hip.

Making the pattern smaller

To shorten the pattern above the waist work out how much shorter you want and fold off this amount along the upper horizontal lines. To shorten it below the waist, fold along the lower line.

To make the pattern narrower, work out the difference you want in size and divide by four (this is because you are cutting two layers from each pattern piece). Fold off this amount along the vertical line on both the back and front sections. Re-shape the neckline.

Enlarging the pattern

Use the same broken lines, but instead of folding cut along the relevant broken lines and spread the pattern by the required amount.

Lay the pattern pieces on a large sheet of paper and spread them until you have the right size. Be sure to cut and spread each piece separately or you may mix them up. Pin the pieces on the paper. Pencil around the outline.

Unpin the pieces, transfer the marks for the darts and pockets onto the new outline and cut out the new pattern.

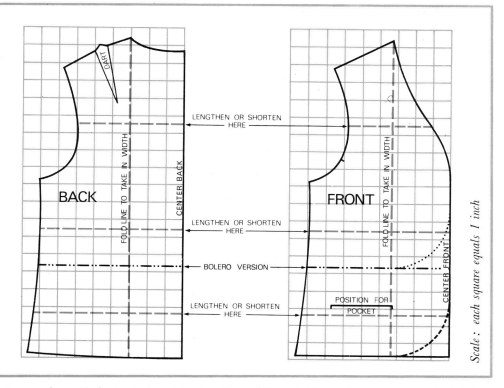

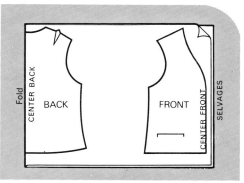

▲ *Layout for vest on 54 inch wide fabric*

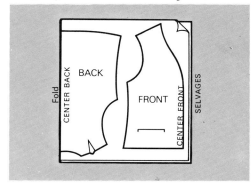

▲ *Layout on 36 inch wide fabric without one way*

Scale : each square equals 1 inch

Pattern on the graph for the back and front sections of the vest. Seam allowances are not included

Choosing the fabric and working out the yardage

It is important to choose a fabric which will hold its shape, particularly for an edge-to-edge vest, which would hang limply if it were made in a flimsy fabric. The patterns are small enough to use up remnants, but if you are buying a length of fabric, work out the yardage on paper as for the skirt. Take a piece of paper half the width of the fabric and lay out the patterns as shown in the diagram.

Pencil in the lines and add ½ inch seam allowances all around. Measure the overall length of the paper to give you the amount of fabric you require.

The edge-to-edge vest is fully lined and needs the same amount of lining fabric.

Cutting out the fabric

Using the paper layout from which you calculated the fabric length, fold the fabric and lay the pattern on it, with the center back on the fold. Add ½ inch seam allowances all around and cut out.

Cut out the lining in the same way, but with ⅜ inch seam allowances only. You will see the reason for this later.

Making the vest

On the outside fabric baste the shoulder darts, side and shoulder seams. Fit, make the necessary adjustments, then stitch. Baste and stitch the lining in the same way, including any alterations you may have made to the outside fabric.

With right sides facing and outer edges even, lay the lining against the outside fabric. Using the seamline of the outside fabric, pin and baste them together around the neck, fronts and lower edge. Leave the armhole edges just pinned.

You will notice that you have to ease the outside fabric onto the lining a little. This is because the lining has been cut slightly smaller to prevent it from showing from underneath when the vest is turned to the right side.

Stitch the two fabrics together along the basted edge. It is easier to work with the lining uppermost so that the slight fullness in the outside fabric can work into the seams.

Do not stitch the armhole seams.

Remove the basting thread on the stitched seams. Trim across the corners and snip the seam allowance around back of neck. Unpin the armhole seams and pull the garment to the right side through one of the armholes.

Baste around the stitched edges.

You will notice that the lining is pulling the edge to the inside of the garment a little. This is correct and is the result of cutting the lining slightly smaller.

Press the edges gently.

To finish the armhole seam

On a loose garment such as a vest the armhole edge has to bear a lot of strain and wear, so it must be given a good firm finish.

Pin and baste the top and lining firmly together around the armhole edges. Measure around the armhole, and from the left-over lining fabric cut a 2 inch wide bias strip 2 inches longer than the armhole measurement.

Following the instructions for armhole facings in Dressmaking chapter 11, page 216, curve the strip and stitch it in place as for the dress. For additional strength stitch over the seam again, starting halfway between shoulder and underarm around the underarm curve and halfway up the back, and finish the facing as before. Finish the other armhole in the same way.

Making the pocket flaps

Cut two strips of fabric 3½ inches wide, to the length indicated on the pattern. Add ½ inch at each end.

If necessary, trim the outside of the pockets now to match the trimming on the vest.

Fold one strip in half lengthwise, right sides facing. Taking ½ inch seams, stitch the strip together all around, leaving a 1 inch opening in center of long edge.

Trim the seams and snip across the corners.

Turn the strip to the right side through the opening. Baste along the stitched edges, then close the opening with small slip stitches.

Make the other pocket in the same way. Pin and baste the pocket flaps to the vest and sew in place with small slip stitches.

Fashion Flair

Skills with scarves

Most of us associate the word scarf with the straggly knitted object which was part of our winter gear. But if you can recover from your childhood complex, you will discover an indispensable fashion accessory which adapts ad infinitum to give any outfit a touch of fashion flair. Get started on the ideas shown here.

Creative Hint. If you're planning to make a fake fur scarf, cut with very sharp scissors, or if the hair is thick, use a single-edged razor blade on the backing only. Finish the edges with tape. Place tape on fur side, overcast with small stitches and miter corners. Turn tape to backing side and anchor with long basting stitches. Attach the lining to the tape.

1. *Contrast fabrics by wearing a soft, silky scarf with a thick woolen coat and slot it through the belt.*
2. *Wear a long, thick-knit scarf, deeply fringed, with a long coat.*
3. *Knot a long, printed silk scarf firmly at the nape of the neck, Romany style, and let the ends flow free. Great emergency cover-up for lanky locks, too.*
4. *Make a luxury scarf with one side suede, one Mongolian fake fur.*
5. *Make a change from a belt by wearing a skinny neck scarf around the hips of a tunic.*
6. *Use a length of fake fur like a scarf with a slim dress.*

Pattern Library

Three-dimensional diamonds

Half cushion stitch is one of those geometrically shaped stitches which can be used to produce some unusual effects if contrasting colors are used for each half of the cushion stitch square.

The diamond pattern illustrated here uses bright red and three contrasting greens; if the design were worked in closely related tones of the same color, a three-dimensional effect would be achieved. Groups of toning colors would give an interesting optical effect if used so

that the diamond shapes near the edge of the work are in the darkest shades and those near the center in the palest shades. Try using yarns of contrasting texture, such as wool and plastic raffia, but of similar colors for each complete cushion square for a fascinating checkerboard effect.

Knitting Know-how 24

Woven looks for knits

Working with a favorite knitting pattern, interesting textures and a woven fabric effect can be achieved by substituting these simple "woven knitting" stitches for stockinette stitch and garter stitch. Because the stitches are based on multiples of two, they are easily adapted to patterns based on an even number of stitches. The gauge of these stitches is likely to be different from stockinette or garter stitch and you should work a test swatch and change the needle size if necessary until the gauge given in the pattern is obtained. Both sides of these woven knitting stitches can be used as the pattern. An unusual and interesting effect could be achieved by using both sides of a stitch in one design, such as a panel down the front of a sweater or dress.

Woven diagonal rib stitch
Worked over an even number of sts, plus 2 edge sts.
1st row. K.
2nd row. K1, *ytf, sl 1P, K1, rep from * to last st, K1.
3rd row. K1, *K1, K2 tog tbl, thus working together the slipped and the yo made on previous row, rep from * to last st, K1.
4th row. K1, *K1, ytf, sl 1P, rep from * to last st, K1.
5th row. K1, *K2 tog tbl, thus working together the slipped and the yo made on previous row, K1, rep from * to last st, K1.
Rows 2-5 form the pattern and are repeated throughout.

Just for inspiration! Knit a skirt and top in any of the woven fabric stitches given in this chapter ►
◄ *The reverse of woven diagonal rib stitch. Both sides of fabric stitches can be used effectively.*
▼ *Woven diagonal rib stitch*

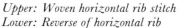

Upper: Plain woven stitch
Lower: Reverse of plain woven

Upper: Woven vertical rib stitch
Lower: Reverse of woven vertical rib

Upper: Woven horizontal rib stitch
Lower: Reverse of horizontal rib

Upper: Woven herringbone stitch
Lower: Reverse of woven herringbone

Plain woven stitch

Worked over an even number of sts, plus 2 edge sts.
1st row. K.
2nd row. K1, *ytf, sl 1 knitwise, rep from * to last st, K1.
3rd row. K1, *K2 tog tbl, thus working together the slipped and the yo made on previous row, rep from * to last st, K1.
The 2nd and 3rd rows form pattern and are repeated throughout.

Woven vertical rib stitch

Worked over an even number of sts, plus 2 edge sts.
1st row. K1, *ytf, sl 1 knitwise, K1, rep from * to last st, K1.
2nd row. K1, *K1, K2 tog tbl, thus working together the slipped and the yo made on previous row, rep from * to last st, K1.
These 2 rows form the pattern and are repeated throughout.

Woven horizontal rib stitch

Worked over an even number of sts, plus 2 edge sts.
1st row. K.

2nd row. P.
3rd row. K1, *insert right-hand needle between next 2 sts on left-hand needle and draw st through, K first st on left-hand needle, rep from * to last st, K1.
4th row. K1, *P2 tog, rep from * to last st, K1.
These 4 rows form the pattern and are repeated throughout.

Woven herringbone stitch

Worked over an even number of sts.
1st row. K2 tog tbl, but drop only the first loop off the left-hand needle, *K the st rem on left-hand needle tog tbl with the next st on left-hand needle, again dropping only the first loop off the needle, rep from * until 1 loop rem on left-hand needle, K1 tbl.
2nd row. P2 tog, dropping only the first loop off the left-hand needle, *P the st rem on left-hand needle tog with the next st on left-hand needle, again dropping only the first loop off the needle, rep from * until 1 loop rem on left-hand needle, P1.
These 2 rows form the pattern and are repeated throughout.

463

Viva el poncho!

Cover yourself with the gaucho look in this magnificent tassel-trimmed poncho, worked here in a soft nylon and wool mixture yarn.

Choose a brilliant single color or, for an authentic Peruvian look, work the pattern in alternating brown and white bands.

Size

Directions fit 32-40in bust.

Gauge

Approx. 7sc and 2 rows crossed clusters and 4 rows sc over 2in

---

Materials

Reynolds Versailles
10 50 gr balls
One No.H (5.00 mm)
crochet hook
One set of four No.5 (or
Canadian No.8) double-
pointed needles

Poncho

Ch120.
Join to form a circle with a ss into the first ch.

1st round Ch2 to form first st, skip first ch, *1sc into each ch to end. Join with a ss into 2nd of first 2ch. 120sc including first st.

2nd round Ch2 to form first st, skip first sc, *1sc into each of next 30sc, ch2, rep from * 3 times more. Join with a ss into 2nd of first 2ch.

3rd round Ch2, 1sc into first sc, *1sc into each of next 30sc, into ch2 sp work 1sc, ch2, 1sc, rep from * twice more, 1sc into each of next 30sc, into ch2 sp work 1sc, ch2. Join with a ss into 2nd of first 2ch.

464

4th round Ch2, 1sc into first sc, *1sc into each of next 32sc, into ch2 sp work 1sc, ch2, 1sc, rep from * twice more, 1sc into each of next 32sc, into next ch2 sp work 1sc, ch2. Join with a ss into 2nd of first 2ch.

5th round As 4th, working 34sc between corners instead of 32.

6th round Ch3, 1dc into last ch2 sp worked, *skip 2sc, 2dc into next sc, 1sc into 2nd of 2 skipped sc, forming a crossed cluster with the 2dc already worked, rep from * 11 times, into corner ch2 sp work 2dc, ch2, 2dc, rep from * to last corner working 2dc, ch2 into ch2 sp. Join with a ss into 3rd of first 3ch.

7th round As 6th, noting that there will be one more crossed cluster on each side than on the previous round.

8th round Ch2, skip first dc, *1sc into each st to corner ch2 sp, ch2, rep from * 3 times more. Join with a ss into 2nd of first 2ch.

9th round Ch2, 1sc into first sc, *1sc into each sc to corner ch2 sp, into ch2 sp work 1sc, ch2, 1sc, rep from * twice more, 1sc into each sc to last ch2 sp, into ch2 sp work 1sc, ch2. Join with a ss into 2nd of first 2ch.

10th-11th rounds As 9th. Continue in this way, gradually increasing and working 2 rows of cluster patt alternately with 4 rows sc, until there are 8 patt panels and 9sc panels.

Last round Ch2, skip first sc, 1sc into next sc, *ch2, skip 2sc, 1sc into each of next 2sc, rep from * along all

4 edges. Join with a ss into 2nd of first 2ch.
Finish off.

This row of loops forms the base for the fringe, one tassel being worked into each loop.

Fringe

Cut lengths of yarn about 7in long. Take 5 strands and fold in half. With crochet hook draw loop at fold through one loop of last row. Draw loose ends of tassel through loop of tassel and draw up tightly.

Continue in this way into each loop around lower edge. Trim the ends of the fringe if required.

Neck

Using set of four No.5 needles, with RS of work facing, pick up and K 120sts along first round of crochet.

Arrange sts evenly on 3 needles and work the collar in rounds as follows:

Work 25 rounds K2, P2 rib.
K 2 rounds.
P 2 rounds.
Rep last 4 rounds twice more.
K 1 round.

Next round *K15, M1K, rep from * to end.
128 sts.
Work 12 rounds K2, P2 rib.
Bind off in rib.

Stand out in a crowd in bright red ►
▼ *Detail of crossed cluster stitch*

Striking looks in straw

Informal table settings take on a festive look with table mats and napkin holders in different sizes and shapes crocheted in straw.

Materials
Straw Yarn
Large blue mat 9 skeins
Small blue mat 3 skeins
Blue napkin holder 1 skein
Large gold mat 6 skeins
Small gold mat 2 skeins
Gold napkin holder 1 skein
One No.F (4.00 mm) crochet hook

Large blue mat

Ch40.
1st row Into 3rd ch from hook work 1dc, *1dc into next ch, rep from *·to end. Turn.
2nd row Ch3, skip first dc, *1dc into next dc, rep from * to end, working last dc into turning ch. Turn. (38dc including turning ch.)
Rep 2nd row 22 times more.

Edging
1st round Ch3, 3dc into same st as ch, work 48dc evenly spaced along first side to corner, 4dc into corner, work 36dc along 2nd side, 4dc into corner, 48dc along 3rd side, 4dc into corner and 36dc along 4th side. Join with a ss into 3rd of first 3ch.
2nd round 1sc between center 2dc in corner, ch4, *skip 3dc, 1sc between next dc, ch4, rep from * to end. Be very careful at each corner to work into the center. Join with a ss into first sc.
3rd round Work 5sc into each ch4 loop to end.
4th round Ss across first

2sc, 1sc into 3rd sc of loop, ch4, *1sc into 3rd sc of next loop, ch4, rep from * to end. Join with a ss into first sc.
5th round Work 5sc into each ch4 loop. Join with a ss into first sc.
Fasten off.

Small blue mat

Ch27.
1st row Into 3rd ch from hook work 1dc, *1dc into next ch, rep from * to end. Turn.
2nd row Ch3, skip first dc, *1dc into next dc, rep from * to end, working last dc into turning ch. Turn. (25dc including turning ch.)
Rep 2nd row 3 times more.

Edging
1st round Ch3, 3dc into same st as ch, work 10dc evenly spaced along first side, 4dc into corner, work 23dc along 2nd side, 4dc into corner, 10dc along 3rd side, 4dc into corner and 23dc along 4th side. Join with a ss into 3rd of first 3ch.
Work 2nd-5th rounds as given for large mat.
Fasten off.

Blue napkin holder

Ch28.
1st round Into 3rd ch from hook work 1dc, *1dc into next ch, rep from * to end, ch2, 1ss into end of commencing ch, ch3, turn the work and work 1dc into opposite side of commencing ch to end, ch3, 1sc on end of ch between the dc rows, ch2, 1ss into top of first st.
2nd round *Ch5, skip 3dc, 1sc between next dc, rep

from * to end, ch5 across end, 1sc into top of first st, rep along 2nd side and end in same way. Join with a ss into base of first loop.
3rd round Work 5sc into each ch loop along each side and end. Join with a ss into first sc.
Fasten off.

Large gold mat

Ch22.
1st round Into 2nd ch from hook work 1sc, *1sc into next ch, rep from * to last ch, 3sc into last ch. Turn and work along the other side of commencing ch, working 2sc into last ch. (same as ch as first sc). Join with a ss into first st.
2nd round Ch3, 2dc into same st as first ch, *skip 2sc, 3dc into next sc, rep from

* to end of side. Work 3dc into center end st and work other side in same way. Join with a ss into 3rd of first 3ch.
3rd round Turn work so that the reverse side is facing, 1sc, ch2 into first space to left between first and 2nd 1dc of central 3dc group, 2dc into same space, skip 1dc, 3dc into next space, skip 1dc, *3dc into next space, ch1, rep from * along side to end, 3dc, ch1 into each space between dc of central group, complete as for other side. Join with a ss into 2nd of first 2ch. There will be 7 groups of 3dc between 4 end groups of 3dc.
4th round Turn and work on the other side, 1sc, ch2 into next space between the 3rd and 4th dc group at one end, 2dc into same space,

The small blue mat measures 7in by 12in, the larger 16½in by 16½in

3dc into each space between dc groups to end. Join with a ss into 2nd of first 2ch.

5th round As 3rd.

6th round As 4th.

7th round As 3rd.

8th round As 4th, working ch1 between each dc group.

9th round Turn and work on the reverse side, 1sc, ch2 into first of 2 central spaces, 2dc into same space, skip 1dc, 3dc into next space, work 4 groups of 3dc into next 4 spaces, work 3dc between each dc of next group, work 7 groups of 3dc into next 7 spaces, work 3dc between each dc of next group, work 4 groups of 3dc into next 4 spaces, work 3dc between each dc of next group, work 4 groups of 3dc into next 4 spaces, work 3dc between each dc of next group, work 7 groups of 3dc into next 7 spaces, work 3dc between each dc of next group, work 4 groups of 3dc into next 4 spaces. Join with a ss into 2nd of first 2ch.

10th round As 8th.

11th round As 8th.

12th round Turn work as before, 1sc, ch2 into first space to left, *1dc into space between groups, 1dc into each of first 2dc of next group, ch4, 1sc into first ch to form picot, 1dc into same st as last dc, 1dc into 3rd dc of group, rep from * to end. Join with a ss into 2nd of first 2ch. Fasten off.

Small gold mat

Ch11.
Work 1st to 6th rounds as for large mat.

Next round Work as given for 12th round of large mat.

Note On the 3rd round there will be 3 groups of 3dc between 4 end groups of 3dc.

Gold napkin holder

Ch22.

1st row Into 2nd ch from hook work 1sc, *1sc into next ch, rep from * to end. Turn.

2nd row Ch2, *skip 2sc, 3dc into next sc, rep from * 5 times more, skip 2sc, 1dc into last sc, ch2, 1sc into end of commencing ch, ch2, 1dc into first dc at other side of commencing ch, * skip 2sc, 3dc into next sc, rep from * 5 times more, skip 2sc, 1dc into last st, ch2, 1sc into center row, ch2. Join with a ss into 2nd of first 2ch.

3rd row Ch2, 1sc into space before first 3dc group, *1sc between first and 2nd dc of next group, ch4, 1sc into first ch to form picot, 1sc between 2nd and 3rd dc of same group, 1sc into space before next group, rep from * along side, work 3sc into end space, ch4 and picot, 3sc into next space, work the other side and end in same way. Fasten off.

Finishing

Darn in all ends securely. Place all pieces flat under a damp cloth and press with a warm iron. Form the holders into a circle by overlapping the ends and fastening with small stitches.

▼ *The oval-shaped gold mats are made using an all-over lacy pattern. With a set of matching napkin holders they would make delightful gifts.*

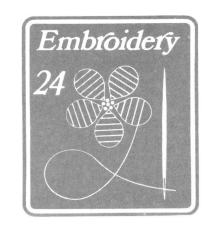

Embroidery 24

Variations on a theme

Decorative, reinforced corners are an important stage in drawn threadwork and the three pretty corner finishes described here will help you to achieve a professional look on your handmade linen.

This chapter describes several attractive variations which can be worked on the basic hemstitch described in Embroidery 21, page 414—ladder hemstitch, zigzag hemstitch and one of the effects obtained by knotting groups of threads. With a little imagination, you will be able to work out your own variations by using different yarns and by grouping and twisting the threads in other ways. Why not dig out an old tablecloth and experiment with some of these ideas?

Decorative, reinforced corners

When two or more rows of threads have been drawn out (as for instance on the tray cloth shown in Embroidery chapter 21), a square empty space is formed at the corners where the drawn threads met. After the ends of the threads have been darned in, the edges of the square are worked very closely with satin stitch or buttonhole stitch to prevent the hole from fraying. With fine fabrics, the hole is very small and may be left with just the edges finished off. With coarse fabrics, the hole is larger and is filled with a worked web to decorate and strengthen the corner. Both dove's eye filling and loop stitch filling are simple to do and form the basis for more complicated and decorative fillings.

Each of these fillings is based on a simple, reinforced corner—a corded or buttonhole-stitched edge is worked very closely along the edges of the square (see illustration).

Dove's eye filling

To work dove's eye filling, fasten the embroidery thread to one corner of the square and take it across diagonally to the opposite corner of the square. Return to center and work in the same way across the other two corners. Where the threads cross, work the dove's eye by stitching around and around until the eye is large enough. Take the thread across to one of the corners and fasten off.

Loop stitch filling

Loop stitch filling, which has a pretty, lacy look, is used when the corner hole is not very large. Follow the diagram (right) for the method of working this simple decorative filling.

Variations on hemstitch

Ladder hemstitch

This simple hemstitch variation is worked where four to six threads have been drawn. Work hemstitch on both sides of exposed thread area, making a series of vertical groupings. Two, three or four threads are taken up by the needle to form the groups.

468

Zigzag hemstitch

Begin this stitch by working a single row of hemstitch, taking up an even number of threads (two, four or six). On the opposite side of the drawn threads, take up half of the same group of threads with half of the adjacent group, making a zigzag effect.

Knotting groups of threads

The knotting of groups of threads produces more attractive variations on ladder hemstitch. Twisted chain stitch is the knot which holds the groups of threads firmly (see the illustration at the bottom of the opposite page), and is obtained by placing the needle as for chain stitch and passing it under the group of threads. The embroidery thread is left visible and forms part of the pattern. You can remove more threads, working more rows of chain stitch to form zigzag patterns.

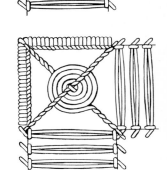

To work dove's eye filling, fasten thread to top left corner of hole and take it across diagonally to bottom right corner. Slip the needle up through the edge stitch to come out at top right and then across diagonally to bottom left. Oversew back along the crossed thread to the top right corner and then slip the needle through the reinforced edge stitching to top left corner. Oversew the thread down to center of crossed threads and weave dove's eye to required size. Oversew the remaining diagonal thread to finish bottom right.

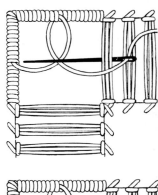

Loop stitch filling is worked by first fixing the thread to the left side of the reinforced hole and then by looping the thread to the upper edge, then to the right edge, then to the lower edge and finishing back on the left (follow the diagram given) ►

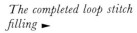

The completed loop stitch filling ►

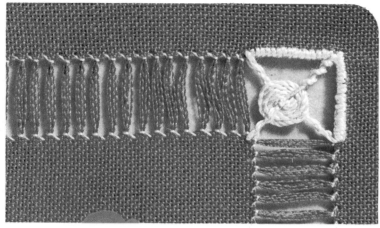

▲*Simple reinforced corner using buttonhole stitch in contrasting color*

▲*Dove's eye filling worked on satin stitch reinforcing in contrast color*

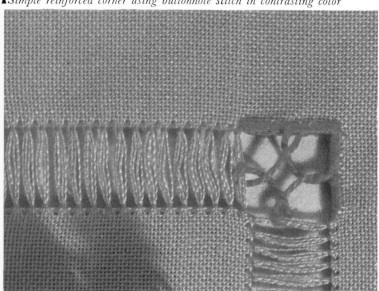

▲ *Loop stitch filling on satin stitch reinforcing in matching thread*
▼ *Zigzag hemstitch worked over groups of four drawn threads*

▲ *Ladder hemstitch worked on both sides of the drawn threads*
▼ *Three groups of threads knotted together with twisted chain stitch*

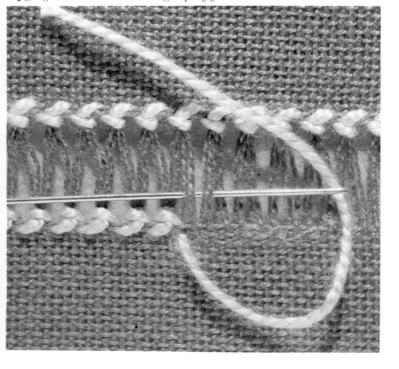

Collector's Piece

The Hastings Embroidery

This embroidery was commissioned by the Borough of Hastings from the Royal School of Needlework in England to celebrate the 900th anniversary of the Battle of Hastings. A team of 18 embroiderers took just over a year to complete the embroidery which consists of 27 panels, each measuring 9 feet by 3 feet, 243 feet in all. They depict important events in British history from the arrival of William the Conqueror to the present day. Shown here are panels nos. 7, 14, 16 and 17.

14th-15th century
At the Battle of Bannockburn in 1314, Robert the Bruce of Scotland defeats Edward II of England. Relations between England and France become hostile, and the year 1337 witnesses the start of the Hundred Years' War.

The French are defeated in 1346 at the Battle of Crécy by the English army under the leadership of Edward III and the Black Prince.

16th-17th century
Queen Elizabeth I commissions Sir Walter Raleigh to found the first colony in America, Virginia. Mary Queen of Scots, accused of originating a plot to assassinate Queen Elizabeth, is found guilty and condemned to death in 1586. The Spanish Armada sails into battle with the English fleet in an attempt to overthrow Elizabeth I's campaign of Protestantism.

17th-18th century
In late summer 1620, the *Mayflower*, with Pilgrims aboard, sets sail for America, where it landed on December 11. Civil war rages in England, the monarchy against Parliament.

The crowd rejoices at the restoration of the monarch in 1660.

17th-19th century
The Great Plague of 1665 ravages London, killing thousands of people. A year later, London is hit by the Great Fire which started in a baker's shop and burned for three days. Many of London's buildings and churches were destroyed, including St. Paul's Cathedral which was rebuilt by Christopher Wren.

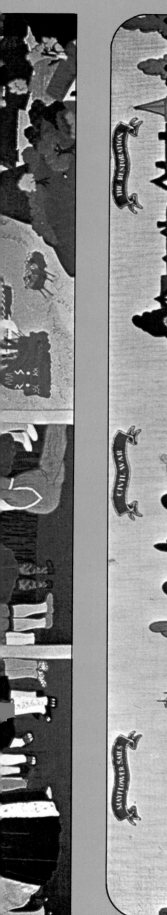

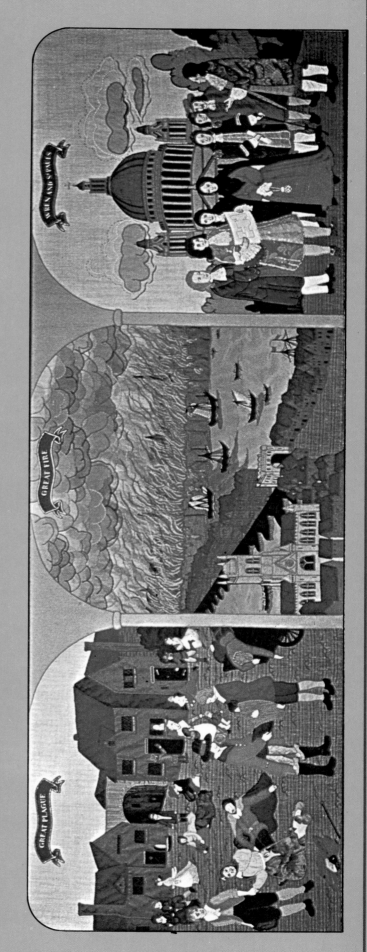

The revival of Florentine stitch

Needle-point 14

Many beautiful and intricate patterns have developed from upright gobelin stitch. One of the most striking of these is the Florentine stitch. These designs were very popular in sixteenth-century Europe, particularly for ecclesiastical embroideries. The most famous examples of this rich, decorative pattern are the upholstered chairs in the Palazzo Vecchio in Florence. Now these beautiful patterns are enjoying a revival and a new popularity because they look so right in both modern and traditional interiors. Turn to the following pages for exciting and unusual gifts to make.

Florentine needlepoint

A Florentine design is made of simple stitches in a zigzag or wavy line formation. The final result depends on the length of the basic stitch, the length of the stepping in the zigzag and the number of stitches in each step.

In this chapter there are three versions of Florentine design. Once you have worked these, the basic principles of Florentine design will become obvious and you will then be able to work out your own patterns quite easily using colored pencils on graph paper. Each line on the grid represents a thread in the canvas.

Florentine design is ideal for anything from handbags and compact cases to stool or chair covers, bolsters and pillows.

Although the overall effect can be complex, the patterns are very simple to work. Once the key line from the chart has been worked right across the canvas, the rest of the pattern is simply a matter of following this line and repeating it in different tones and colors. This type of needlepoint is best worked on single-weave canvas. It is not necessary to work in a frame because the straight stitches used do not pull the canvas out of shape. It is essential, however, to plan the design from the key line positioned across the center of the area to be covered, and then work outward.

Yellow and blue zigzag
Repeat the zigzag key line three times in each of the blue tones and then three times in the tones of yellow. You could, of course, use tones of colors other than blue and yellow. For a bolder effect use only one tone of each of the two main colors, still working in sets of three rows.

Flame pattern
This design looks most effective, and more flame-like, if it is worked in several tones of one color (as illustrated), or in very closely related colors.

Ogee flame pattern
This design is worked in steps, arranged to give a delightfully fluid effect. Try to fit in a complete set of repeats when planning this pattern, otherwise the effect is lost.

472

▲ *Yellow and blue zigzag pattern*

▲ *Flame pattern* *Ogee flame pattern* ▶

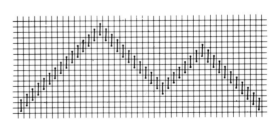

Chart for zigzag pattern key line

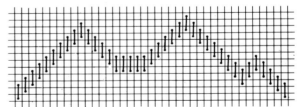

Chart for flame pattern key line

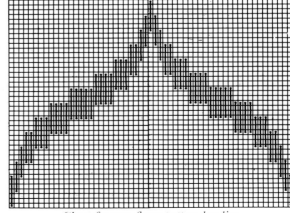

Chart for ogee flame pattern key line

473

Gifts to make

If something is handmade, it is likely to be fairly rare—and expensive. These beautiful personal accessories are an elegant luxury which you can make either to keep for yourself or to give to friends as gay gifts. If you decide to make several of them, you will not need a complete new set of yarns for each one, as there will be yarn left over. When you come to make them, refer to Needlepoint 5, page 112, where you will find full instructions on blocking the worked canvas and the most suitable seaming stitches.

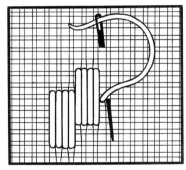

Single-thread canvas or double-thread (10 double threads to the inch) can be used for the Florentine items on these pages. If double-thread canvas is used, work between the vertical threads (see diagram) for the ogee flame pattern used in two of the items.

Key 1	Color	Key 2
⊡	Aquamarine	⊟
▨	Cornflower blue	⊞
⊠	Pale amethyst	⊞
◪	Sage green	⧠
◼	Royal blue	⊞

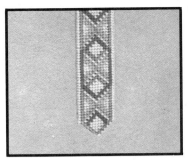

Headband 9½in by 1 7/16in

Headband

You will need
- ☐ Canvas 11in by 3in
- ☐ 5 skeins tapestry yarn, one in each color
- ☐ Lining 11in by 3in
- ☐ Elastic ¼in wide

To work the embroidery
Work the headband in half cross-stitch (Needlepoint chapter 2, page 22) using the colors indicated on the chart. Repeat the pattern until the work measures 9½ in. long. When completed, block the work (see Needlepoint chapter 5).

To finish
Cut off spare canvas five threads from the edge of the work. Trim the lining material to the same size. Turn excess canvas to the back of the work, mitering the corners. Make turnings on the lining and attach the lining to the canvas, wrong sides facing. Slip stitch along the long edges. Cut a length of the elastic and slot the ends into the open ends of the headband, between canvas and lining. Stitch firmly into place. Slip stitch to close ends.

Chart for working the headband

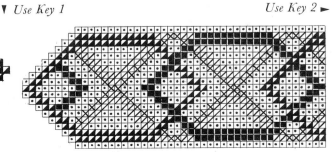

Belt with clasp buckle

Belt

You will need
- ☐ Canvas to fit waist measurement (see below)
- ☐ 5 skeins tapestry yarn
- ☐ Lining material (as canvas)
- ☐ Strong, prongless buckle

Measure your waist and add 2in for ease, 6in overlap to thread through the buckle and 1½in for attaching the buckle. The narrowest belt which can comfortably be made in needlepoint is ¾in, while the widest, without stiffening, is about 2½ in. For a really wide belt, allow further ease to the belt length and use stiff interfacing. For a clasp buckle as shown in photo above, omit the 6in overlap at the end of the belt.

To work the embroidery
Work the belt in half cross-stitch in the colors on the chart. Repeat this pattern until the canvas has been covered.

To finish
Line the belt as for headband, leaving the buckle end flat, and oversew the edges together. Place the buckle over the end of belt, fold over 1½in and stitch firmly in place.

Chart for the belt end and repeat

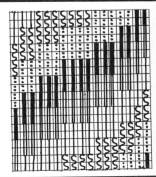

Compact case 3¾in by 3¾in

Compact case

You will need
- ☐ Canvas 9½in by 5½in
- ☐ 5 skeins tapestry yarn, one in each color
- ☐ Lining 9½in by 5in
- ☐ 12in of fine cord

To work the embroidery
Work the compact case in Florentine stitch, using the colors as indicated on the chart, working between the canvas threads for a closer texture (see diagram). Work two patterns across the width of the canvas and continue until the embroidery is 7½in long.

To finish
After blocking, trim excess canvas to within 5 threads of the embroidery, line the work and slip stitch all around. Fold the work in half across the width, pin and whip stitch the edges together (see Needlepoint chapter 5). Leave ¼in open at the lower corners to tuck in the ends of cord. Slip stitch the cord up one side across the top and down the other side. Secure the cord firmly at the corners.

Chart for working the compact case

▼ *Use Key 1*

Use Key 2 ►

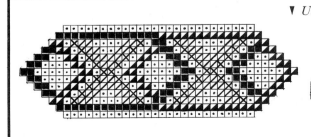

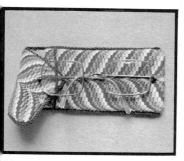

Glasses case 6½in by 2¾in

Lighter case 2¾in by 2½in

Glasses case

You will need
☐ Canvas 19in by 7in
☐ 5 skeins tapestry yarn, one in each color
☐ Lining 19in by 7in
☐ 24in of fine cord

To work the embroidery
Work the glasses case in Florentine stitch, using the colors indicated on the chart. Work until the embroidery measures 14½in by 2¾in.

To finish
Block and trim the canvas. Cut the lining to the same size. Attach the lining to the needlepoint with the wrong sides together and slip stitch the edges. Fold the work across the width, ½in from the end, and slip stitch the two side seams, leaving ¼in open at the corners. Tuck the cord end into a corner and stitch in place round case. Cut a piece of cord 3½in long to secure the flap. Tuck the ends of the cord into the side seams at the mouth of the pocket and stitch them in place. The flap tucks under this cord to keep the case closed.

Lighter case

You will need
☐ Canvas 9in by 5in
☐ 5 skeins tapestry yarn
☐ Lining 9in by 5in
☐ 12in of fine cord

To work the embroidery
Work the lighter case in half cross-stitch or tent stitch in the Florentine pattern indicated, following the colors on the chart. Work until the embroidered area measures 2¾in by 6in.

To finish
Block the canvas and trim off the excess. Cut the lining to the same size as the needlepoint and attach the lining as instructed for the headband. Fold the work in half and stitch the side seams, leaving ¼in open at the corners for inserting the ends of cord.
Insert the ends of the cord into the corners and sew the cord neatly into place on three sides of the case, leaving one of the openings without trim.
N.B. For all the items you can, if you wish, make handmade cords using one or more of the yarns used in the embroidery.

Chart for the glasses case

Chart for the lighter case

◄ *Use Key 2*
▼ *Use Key 1*

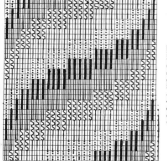

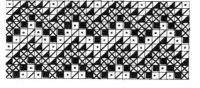

All buttoned up

Creative Hands dressmaking patterns are nothing if not versatile! This crisp, buttoned vest is adapted from the edge-to-edge vest pattern in the previous chapter. It's very simple to convert, easy to make, and provides a practical, tailored-looking garment to coordinate with simple skirts.

▼ *Match a buttoned vest to a simple flared skirt for an attractive outfit*

The pattern

Make the pattern for the hip-length vest with the squared lower front edge following the instructions given in Dressmaking chapter 23, page 454. Also incorporate the necessary size alterations. To make the center front extension, lay the front pattern piece on a sheet of paper with the center front parallel to and 2¾ inches from one edge of the paper. Draw around the pattern and transfer all the pattern details. Following the diagram, draw in the extension line 1 inch below the armhole, across the front of the pattern to the edge of the paper, then draw in the new neckline to meet it. Also extend the hemline. Cut out the new pattern.

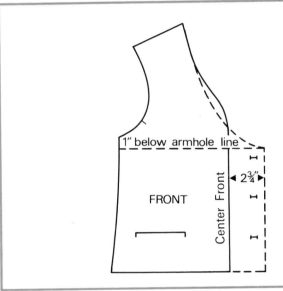

1. *Extending the basic vest for the buttoned version*

Making the facings

Since this vest is buttoned, it does not need a lining. The edges are finished with facings.

To make the facings, lay the pattern pieces on a sheet of paper and pencil around the outside edges. Then copy the inner facing line from the diagram. Cut out the facing patterns.

2. *How to mark out the facings for the buttoned vest*

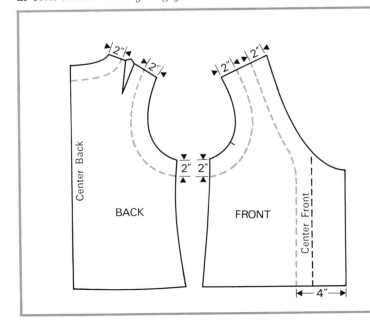

Fabric requirements

54in wide fabric. One and a half times the length, plus 7 inches for seam and hem allowances.

36in wide fabric. Three times the length, plus 12 inches for seam and hem allowances.

You will also need 6 buttons.

Cutting out

Following the appropriate layout, place the pattern pieces on the fabric with the back and back neck facings along a fold. Mark out $\frac{1}{2}$ inch seam and 2 inch hem allowances. For the front facings mark out 2 inches for the hem and make facing seam allowances $\frac{1}{16}$ inch smaller than the vest seam allowance. Facings, like linings, go to the inside of a garment and are therefore cut slightly smaller so that they will stay put and not work out.

Cut out the vest.

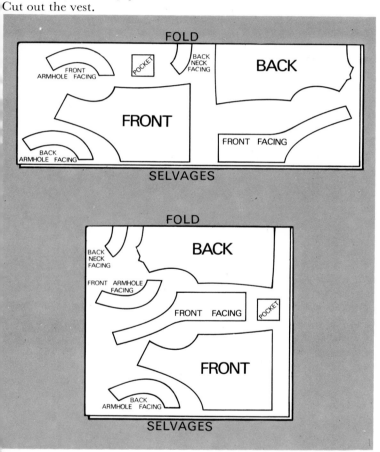

3. Top: layout on 36in wide fabric. Bottom: layout on 54in wide fabric

Making the vest

Stitching the seams and facings

Pin, baste and fit the vest, making the necessary alterations. Stitch the shoulder darts and the shoulder and underarm seams. Press. Stitch the back and front armhole facings together along the shoulder and underarm seams. Stitch the back neck facing to both front facings along the shoulder seams. Press.

With right sides together, lay the facings in position with the outer raw edges even and the shoulder and underarm seams matching. Pin in place, easing the vest onto the facings. Baste together along the vest seamlines. With the facings uppermost, stitch them in place along the basted vest seamlines and not along the facing seamlines.

Snip the seam allowance at the curves.

Topstitching the facings

On garments designed for hard wear, the facings can be topstitched to the seam allowance.

Stitch along the seamlines of the facings, making sure that both seam allowances are turned toward the facing and that you catch them in as you stitch (see diagram 5).

After topstitching the facings you will see how neatly the edges roll toward the inside and that the seam edges are hidden completely. Baste the faced edges to the inside of the vest and press them in position.

Finish off the raw edges of the facings and seams, overcasting them by hand. Lightly sew the facing edges to the seams only.

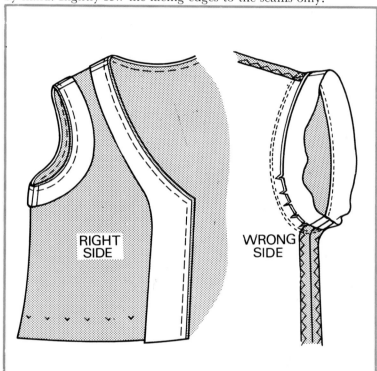

4. The basted facings   **5.** Topstitched facing

The hem

Open out the facings at the lower edge of the vest. Turn up the hem and sew in place working right along the facings. Then fold the facings back over the hem and slip stitch in position over the hem allowance and along the lower edge.

Buttons, buttonholes and pockets

Use diagram 1 as a guide to placing the buttonholes, being careful to rearrange the spacing if you have altered the size of the pattern. Make the buttonholes as shown in Dressmaking chapter 19, page 368, ¾ inch from the front edge.

Sew on the buttons. Match the center front lines and sew the first row to correspond with the buttonholes. Place and sew the second row of buttons the same distance from the front edge, opposite the buttonholes.

Make and stitch on the pockets as shown in Dressmaking 23, p 454.

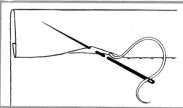

Slip stitch
This stitch gives an invisible finish and is worked in an almost straight line as opposed to the zigzag motion of a felling or hemming stitch.

What your sewing machine can do

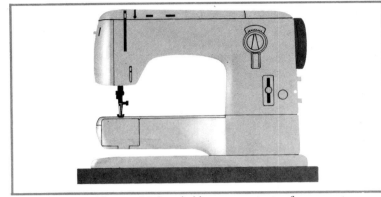

▲ *A free arm machine, useful for stitching narrow parts of a garment*

Sewing machines can produce exciting effects, in a few minutes, which would take hours of working by hand. Their potential was briefly described in Dressmaking chapter 1, page 28, but there are many more things today's machines can do. This chapter sets out to help you find which type you want, and since buying a sewing machine is a critical business, it's important to assess your needs before making a choice.

Buying a sewing machine?

Before buying a sewing machine, you should ask yourself the following questions:
a. How much do you expect from your machine?
b. How much sewing do you do?
c. How much are you prepared to spend?

Choose a machine to suit your needs

When buying a sewing machine you should consider the various electric models on the market and choose the one with the facilities you are going to need.

A straight-stitch machine is only capable of straight machining, which means that all overcasting, finishing and buttonhole making has to be done by hand.

All that most people need for everyday dressmaking is a sewing machine with a good straight stitch and a reverse for ending off seams, a zigzag stitch with adjustable width, and an attachment for making neat buttonholes. A machine which does stretch stitching and basting is also an advantage.

However, the more a machine can do, the more expensive it is, and it is pointless to spend money on attachments you will never use. A swing-needle or zigzag machine saves a lot of time, and is therefore worth the extra cost. Apart from the usual straight stitch, swing-needle machines have a manual control knob for engaging a zigzag setting, and both the stitch length and width can be varied. With practice, all sorts of uses for this machine can be discovered, particularly overcasting and working buttonholes.

Read this chapter carefully, noting the points which apply to your particular dressmaking requirements, then set about finding a machine which answers your needs and is also in your price bracket.

Special attachments

Apart from the general-purpose foot on your machine, a zipper foot and a buttonhole foot are the most useful attachments.

The zipper foot. This is constructed to enable you to stitch right up to a zipper edge without the zipper teeth being under the presser foot. The zipper foot is usually provided with a new sewing machine as part of the purchase. When buying a zipper foot, make sure that it is for your particular make of machine.

The buttonhole foot and button plate. Some buttonhole feet are specially grooved so that the buttonhole can pass underneath.

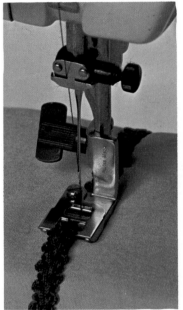

▲ *Special foot for narrow braiding*
▼ *Lace trim stitched with zigzag*

▲ *Special zipper foot in action*
▼ *Programmed scalloping cuff trim*

▼ *Fine pin-tucking on a cuff*

▼ *Fine zigzag for frills*

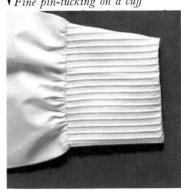

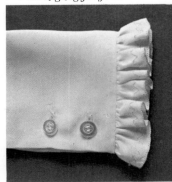

Programmed machine embroidery

▲ *Machined tailor's tacks*

Pin tucks, eyelets and scalloping

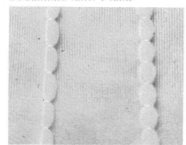

▲ *Shell edging on fine fabric*

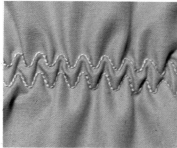

▲ *Serpentine stitched elastic*

It helps if the foot is made of plastic, as you can see the work through it. The button plate is for stitching on buttons, which may be helpful if you have a lot to attach, but hand-sewing is usually sufficient.

Other useful features

Hems. The rolled hem foot is ideal for edging scarves and for very fine rolled hems on chiffon. The foot does all the work for you by rolling and stitching in one operation. There is also a blind hemming or blind stitch foot for making hems on medium-weight fabrics. But, on the whole, hems should be worked by hand.

Darning. A darning foot and plate for darning household linen and clothes.

Gathering and shirring. Most machines have a special foot which will gather and shir all fabrics.

Tailor's tacks. As you can see from the photograph, there are machines which make tailor's tacks like the hand-worked version.

Bias binding. The binder foot stitches on the bias binding and binds the raw edge in one operation.

Running stitch or 3-point zigzag. This stitch is ideal for stitching fabrics which fray easily, like linen or any loosely woven fabric, and is also used on stretch toweling. It has the function of a neatening stitch. The serpentine stitch is similar to the 3-point zigzag and is used for stitching on elastic as shown here.

Sewing for decoration

Many machines today do some embroidery, and a quick look at the machine manual will tell you all you need to know about this.

Some have disks or cams which are inserted into the machine and contain the blueprint of the pattern, while others have a dialling system programmed into the machine.

As you can see in the photographs, there are other methods of decorating with a sewing machine. For instance, on the cuffs shown here, a narrow zigzag stitch is used to edge a fine fabric and to stitch on lace. Here are some other useful decorating effects:

Pin-tucking. A special grooved tucker foot used with twin needles was used for the example shown on this page. The spacing of the tucks can be easily varied.

Eyelet foot and plate. This is for making eyelets, as shown in the photograph.

Shell edging. A special programmed stitch was used for the shell edging in the example.

Free arm or flat bed machine

Having decided what you want your machine to do and the type you are going to buy, you then have to choose between a free arm and a flat bed machine. The difference between these two machines is slight. The free arm is usually a little more expensive and is available in a variety of models. It can be useful when you are stitching narrow parts of a garment, such as sleeves and cuffs, and particularly if you are going to flat-fell the seams, as these sections will fit around the arm of the machine. All free arm machines have a special plate which you can put around the arm to make a flat bed for supporting the work.

Sewing classes

Having bought a new sewing machine you will want to make full use of it. Many companies give free lessons on how to use their machines, and these lessons are worth attending.

Summing up

The chart on the left covers all the special features discussed in this chapter and will help you to see at a glance the type of sewing machine which will be the most useful for you.

Type of machine ▶	Straight stitch	Basic zigzag	Zigzag special	Zigzag deluxe
Straight stitch and reverse	✓	✓	✓	✓
Zigzag with adjustable width		✓	✓	✓
Basting	✓	✓	✓	✓
Adjustable stitch length	✓	✓	✓	✓
Zipper foot	✓	✓	✓	✓
Roller foot		✓	✓	✓
Buttonholes and button plate		✓	✓	✓
Rolled hem foot	✓	✓	✓	✓
Blind hemming			✓	✓
Darning		✓	✓	✓
Gathering	✓	✓	✓	✓
Shirring	✓	✓	✓	✓
Tailor's tacks			some	some
Bias binding		✓	✓	✓
Industrial overlocking				some
Running stitch or 3-point zigzag		some	some	some
Serpentine stitch			some	some
Pin tucking		some	✓	✓
Eyelet foot and plate			some	some
Shell edging			✓	✓

Junior fashion flair

Floribunda fowls

There are many delightful ways of using these flowery fowls; as ideas for appliqué, designs for embroidery, and for making felt novelties.

1. *A comfortable mother hen made of double felt with appliquéd flowers from felt scraps, makes a delightful kitchen egg bowl or hot roll basket.*

2. *Enlarge the designs for patterns for friendly nursery pillows, a pajama bag or a wall panel.*

3. *An egg holder made from single felt to brighten the breakfast table. The mother hen appliquéd on linen makes a co-ordinated place mat.*

4. *Cut out in gay printed fabrics, the chick makes an amusing appliqué for children's clothes.*

5. *Mother hen makes an apron pocket and her chick a pocket for children's clothes or babies' bibs.*

Creative Hint. When making hen or chicken shaped pockets for aprons or dresses, cut out the shape in both a contrasting fabric and a lining fabric. Join the two pieces, right sides facing, leaving A—B open. Turn to the right side, press, turn under edge A—B, pin and baste in position. Topstitch, $\frac{1}{8}$ in from edge, C—A—B—D, leaving D—C open for pocket opening. The same method is used for attaching patch pockets.

If the hen is made as a stand-up toy, the oval shape is used for the base, matching A-A and B-B.

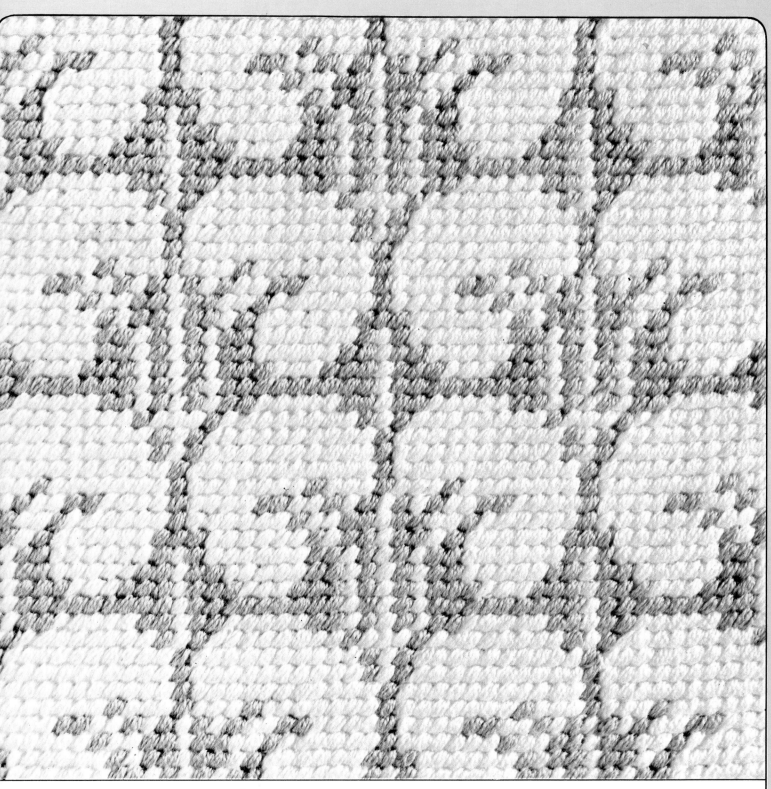

Two color gros point

Pattern Library

This crisp needlepoint design is worked in gros point, which is just like tent stitch but worked over more threads of canvas. In this case each stitch is worked over 3 threads up and 3 threads across.

An all-over pattern such as this is ideal for pillows, handbags, stool or seat covers and needle-made rugs.

Use single-weave canvas with 18 threads to 1in. The design illustrated is worked in D.M.C. Matte Embroidery thread in white and blue 2799.

For chilly days in toytown

Specially for younger knitters, here are Gregor and Sasha again, snug in their new play outfits. Don't they look smart in their cabled turtleneck pullovers and flared pants?

These patterns are an opportunity for you to practice cable stitch—if you want to refresh your memory about how to work it, refer to Knitting Know-how chapter 21, page 402. These patterns are also good practice in blocking and finishing. You will see from chapter 11, page 202 how important it is to sew pieces together in the right manner. There will be more clothes for Gregor and Sasha in later chapters of Knitting Know-how.

For one outfit you will need:

3-ply fingering yarn
Pullover 3 ounces
Pants 2 ounces
One pair No. 2 needles
(or Canadian No. 11)
One pair No. 3 needles
(or Canadian No. 10)

One cable needle

One hook and eye

Gauge
7sts and 9 rows to 1in over stockinette stitch worked on No.3 needles.

Pullover back

Using No.2 needles, cast on 48sts.

Knitting Know-how 25

1st row *K1, P1, rep from * to end.
Rep 1st row 5 times more.
Change to No.3 needles.
Commence patt:
1st row P2, *K4, P4, rep from * to last 6sts, K4, P2.
2nd row K2, *P4, K4, rep from * to last 6sts, P4, K2.
Rep 1st and 2nd patt rows once more.
5th row P2, *sl next 2sts onto cable needle and hold in front of work, K2, K2 from cable needle—called C4F—P4, rep from * to last 6sts, C4F, P2.
6th row As 2nd.
These 6 rows form patt and are rep throughout.
Work 1st-6th rows 5 times more.

Shape armholes
Keeping patt correct, bind off 2sts at beg of next 2 rows.
Dec one st at each end of next 4 rows.
Work 8 rows without shaping.

Shape neck
1st row (RS) Patt 12sts, turn.
**Work 1 row.
Dec one st at neck edge on next 2 RS rows.
Work 1 row.
Bind off 10sts.**
With RS facing, slip center 12 sts onto holder.
Attach yarn to rem sts and patt to end of row.
Complete as given for other side, working from ** to **.

Front

Work as given for back until armhole shaping is complete (36sts). Work 4 rows without shaping.

Shape neck
1st row Patt 12sts, turn.
*** Work 1 row.
Dec one st at neck edge on next 2 RS rows.
Work 5 rows.
Bind off 10sts.***
With RS facing, sl center 12 sts onto holder.
Attach yarn to rem sts.
Work 1 row.
Complete as given for other side from *** to ***.

Sleeves (both alike)

Using No.2 needles, cast on 24sts.
Work 6 rows K1, P1 rib.
Change to No.3 needles.
Work in patt as given for back, inc one st at each end of 7th and every following 6th row until there are 34sts.
Work 5 rows without shaping.

Shape cap
Bind off 2sts at beg of next 2 rows.
Dec one st at each end of every RS row until 20sts rem. Bind off.

Collar

Join left shoulder seam.
With RS facing and No.2 needles, pick up and K 8sts down right back, K12 from back holder, pick up and K 8sts up left back, pick up and K 12sts down left front, K12 from front holder, pick up and K 12sts up right front. Work 20 rows K1, P1 rib. Bind off in rib.

Pants (right leg)

Using No.3 needles, cast on 44sts.
K 4 rows.
5th row Sl 1, P to last st, K1.
6th row Sl 1, K to end.
Rep 5th and 6th rows 3 times more.
13th row Sl 1, P2 tog, P16, P2 tog, P2, P2 tog, P16, P2 tog, K1.
14th row As 6th.
Rep 5th and 6th rows 6 times more.
Next row Sl 1, P2 tog, P14, P2 tog, P2, P2 tog, P14,

P2 tog, K1. Work 7 rows without shaping. Continue inc one st at each end of next and every following 8th row until there are 42sts, then every RS row until there are 50sts. Work 1 row.
Place marker threads at each end of last row to mark beg of body.

Shape body
Bind off 3sts at beg of next 2 rows.**
Dec one st at beg of next and every following 4th row and dec one st at end of next and every following 8th row until 35sts rem. Work 1 row.
Next row K3, P to end.
Next row K.
Rep last 2 rows 4 times more.
Next row K3, *P1, K1, rep from * to end.
Next row *P1, K1, rep from * to last 3sts, K3.
Rep last 2 rows once.
Bind off.

Pants (left leg)

Work as given for right leg to **.
Dec one st at beg of next and every 8th row and dec one st at end of next and every 4th row until 35sts rem.
Next row Cast on 3sts, K to end.
Next row P to last 3sts, K3.
Next row K.
Rep last 2 rows 4 times more.
Next row *K1, P1, rep from * to last 3sts, K3.
Next row K4, *P1, K1, rep from * to last st, P1.
Rep last 2 rows once. Bind off.

Finishing

Press pieces under a damp cloth with a warm iron, excluding ribbing.
Pullover Join shoulder and collar seam. Join side and sleeve seams. Sew in sleeves.
Pants Seam legs to marker threads. Sew body seam from back to markers, and front from markers to extra cast-on sts. Sew cast-on sts below knitted edging of right leg. Sew hook and eye at waist to close opening.

483

All-male vest

This comfortable knit vest will be a handsome addition to any man's wardrobe. What's more, it's fun to make!

Sizes

Directions are for 38in chest. The figures in brackets [ ] refer to the 40, 42 and 44in sizes respectively.
Length down center back, 20½[21½:22:23]in.

Gauge

6sts and 8 rows to 1in over stockinette stitch worked on No.5 needles.

Materials

Sports yarn
4[5:5:5] 2 oz. skeins
One pair No. 3 needles (or Canadian No. 10)
One pair No. 5 needles (or Canadian No. 8)
Five buttons
Stitch holder

Back

Using No.5 needles, cast on 119[125:131:137] sts.
1st row K1, *P1, K1, rep from * to end.
2nd row P1, *K1, P1, rep from * to end.
Continue in K1, P1 rib until work measures 11[11½:12:12½]in from beg.

Shape armholes

Bind off 6sts at beg of next 2 rows.
Dec one st at each end of every row until 81[85:89:93] sts rem.
Continue without shaping until armholes measure 5½[6:6:6½]in from beg.
Inc one st at each end of next

and every following 10th row until there are 87[91:95:99] sts.
Continue without shaping until armholes measure 9½[10:10:10½]in from beg.

Shape shoulders and neck

Next row Bind off 7sts, rib 28[29:30:31], bind off 17 [19:21:23] sts, rib to end.
Complete left shoulder first. Bind off 7sts at armhole edge at the beg of next row, then 7sts every other row twice and 5[6:7:8] sts once; *at the same time* bind off 3sts at neck edge every other row 3 times.
With WS facing, attach yarn to rem sts and work to correspond to first side.

Left front

Using No.5 needles, cast on 3sts.
Commence patt and shaping:
1st row P1, K1, P1.
2nd row Inc in first st (center edge), K to last st, inc in last st (side edge).
3rd row K twice into first st, P1, K1, P1, K twice into last st.
4th row K twice into first st, K to last st, K twice into last st.
Keeping patt correct, inc one st at each end of every row 3[5:7:9] times more.
Continue to inc one st at center edge on every row 12 times more; *at the same time* cast on 9sts at side edge 4 times. 63[67:71:75] sts.
Dec one st at side edge on every 8th row 4 times, then inc one st at this edge on every 6th row 6 times;

at the same time, when inc at center front edge are completed, work even for ¼[½:¾:1]in, ending at center front edge and working a buttonhole on next 2 rows as follows:
Next row Patt 2sts, bind off 2sts, patt to end.
Next row Patt to last 2sts, cast on 2sts, patt 2sts.
Work 4 more buttonholes in this way at intervals of 2½ [2½:2½:2¾]in measured from center of previous buttonhole.
Work until side edge measures 10½[11:11½:12]in from beg, ending at side edge.

Shape armhole and front

Next row Bind off 6sts, patt to last 2sts, work 2 tog.
Dec one st at neck edge on every following 3rd row 21[22:23:24] times more; *at the same time* dec one st at armhole edge on every row 14[16:18:20] times.
Continue until armhole measures 5½[6:6:6½]in from beg, ending at armhole edge.
Inc one st at beg of next and every following 10th row 3 times in all. Continue until armhole measures same as back to shoulder, ending at armhole edge.

Shape shoulder

Bind off at beg of next and every other row 7sts 3 times and 5[6:7:8] sts once.

Right front

Work as given for left front, reversing all shaping and omitting buttonholes.

Finishing

Press lightly.
Join shoulder seams using backstitch.
Armbands Using No.3 needles, RS facing, pick up and K 102[108:108:114] sts evenly around armhole. K 2 rows. Bind off.
Right front edge Using No.3 needles, beg at side edge and pick up and K 43 [45:47:49] sts to center point. K 2 rows, inc one st at center point on each row. Bind off. Using No.3 needles, beg at center point and pick up and K 25[27:29:31] along shaped edge, 65[68:71:74] along center front straight edge, 64[67:67:70] along shaped edge of neck and 19[20:21:22] sts to center back neck. K 2 rows, inc one st at center point on each row. Bind off.
Left front edge Using No.3 needles, beg at center back neck and pick up and K 19[20:21:22]sts, 64[67:67:70] along shaped edge of neck, 65 [68:71:74] along center front straight edge and 25 [27:29:31] along shaped edge to center point. K 2 rows, inc one st at center point on each row. Bind off. Using No.3 needles, beg at center point and pick up and K 43[45:47:49] sts to side edge. K 2 rows, inc one st at center point on each row. Bind off.
Join side and armband seams. Join right and left front edges at center point. Buttonhole stitch around buttonholes and sew on buttons.

▼ *The vest front is in rice stitch, giving a fabric effect*

Crochet Know-how 25

More fancy stitches

This chapter shows how groups of stitches can be worked to form intricate and lacy-looking patterns. All the stitches on these pages are open stitches with the exception of lattice stitch, which forms an attractive diamond pattern on a close fabric background.

Any leftover remnants of yarn can be used to practice these stitches, using a No. E (3.50 mm) crochet hook.

Fan stitch
Make a number of chains divisible by 8, plus 1.

1st row. Into 2nd ch from hook work 1sc, work 1sc into each ch to end. Turn.

2nd row. Ch2, 1sc into each sc to end. Turn.

3rd row. Ch5, skip 3sc, *(1dc, ch3, 1dc) into next sc, ch2, skip 3sc, 1dc into next sc, ch2, skip 3sc, rep from * ending with 1dc into last st. Turn.

4th row. Ch2, *2sc into next space, ch1, 5sc into next space between dc, ch1, 2sc into next space, ch1, rep from * ending with 2sc into last space, skip last ch and work 1sc into turning ch. Turn.

5th row. Ch2, 1sc into first sc, ch1, work petals thus: *yoh, insert hook into first sc of 5sc of previous row, yoh, pull through loop, yoh, put hook into same sc, yoh, pull through loop, yoh, put hook into same sc, yoh, pull through loop, yoh, pull through all 7 loops on hook, rep from * into each of next 4sc, ch1, skip 1ch and 2sc, work 1sc into next ch1 space, ch1, skip 2sc and 1ch, rep from * ending with 1sc and skipping last ch. Turn.

6th row. Ch5, *1sc into space between 2nd and 3rd petals of next petal group, ch2, 1sc into space between 3rd and 4th petals, ch2, (1dc, ch2, 1dc) all into next sc between petal groups, ch2, rep from * skipping 2ch and 1dc from last rep. Turn.

7th row. Ch2, 3sc into first space, work 2sc into every space to end, 1sc into 2nd ch of turning ch. Turn.

Rows 2-7 form pattern and are repeated throughout.

Lattice stitch
Make a number of chains divisible by 4, plus 3.

1st row. Into 2nd ch from hook work 1sc, work 1sc into each ch to end. Turn.

2nd row. Ch2, 1sc into each sc to end. Turn.

3rd row. As 2nd.

4th row. Ch2, 1sc into each of next 2sc, insert hook from front to back of work in first st of first row, yoh, draw up long loop, yoh and pull through first loop on hook, skip 4sts on first row, insert hook from front to back in next space, *yoh, draw up long loop, yoh and pull through first loop on hook, yoh and draw through all 3 loops on hook, skip 1sc behind this st, work 1sc into each of next 3sc, insert hook into same space as last loop worked, yoh, draw up loop, yoh and draw through first loop on hook, skip 4sts on first row, insert hook from front to back in next space, rep from *, ending with 3sc. Turn.

Rep 2nd row 3 times more.

8th row. Ch2, 1sc into next sc, insert hook into st formed whe⟨ loops join in 4th row, yoh, draw up loop, yoh and draw throug⟨ first loop on hook, yoh and draw through both loops, skip sc behin⟨ this st, work 1sc into each of next 3sc, *insert hook from front ⟨ back in same place as first loop, yoh, draw up loop, yoh and dra⟨ through first loop on hook, insert hook in st joining next 2 loops ⟨ 4th row, yoh, draw up loop, yoh and draw through first loop ⟨ hook, yoh, draw through all 3 loops on hook, skip 1sc behind this ⟨ work 1sc into each of next 3sc, rep from * to end, with last loo⟨ pulling yarn through first loop on hook, insert hook in last sc ⟨ 4th row, yoh, draw through loop, yoh, draw through all 3 loops ⟨ hook, skip 1sc behind this st, work 1sc into each of next 3sc. Tur⟨
Rep 2nd row 3 times more.

12th row. Ch2, 1sc into next 2sc, insert hook from front to bac⟨ into st formed on 8th row, yoh, draw up loop, yoh, pull throug⟨ first loop on hook, *insert hook into next joining loops in 8th ro⟨ yoh, draw up loop, yoh, draw through first loop on hook, yo⟨ draw through all 3 loops on hook, skip 1sc behind this st, work 1⟨ into each of next 3sc, insert hook in same place, yoh, draw up loo⟨ yoh and draw through first loop on hook, rep from * ending wi⟨ 3sc. Turn.

Rows 5-12 form pattern and are repeated throughout.

Triangle stitch
Make a number of chains divisible by 3, plus 2.

1st row. Into 2nd ch from hook work 1sc, 1sc into each ch to en⟨ Turn.

2nd row. Ch4, *skip 2sc, work 1dc into next sc, insert hook in⟨ 2nd skipped sc behind dc just worked, work 1dc, ch1, rep from ⟨ ending with 1dc. Turn.

3rd row. Ch2, skip first dc, work 1sc into each st to end, endi⟨ with 1sc into 3rd ch of turning ch. Turn.

Rows 2 and 3 form pattern and are repeated throughout.

Crazy stitch
Make a number of chains divisible by 6, plus 2.

1st row. Into 2nd ch from hook work 1sc, *ch2, skip 2ch, wo⟨ 3dc into next ch, ch2, skip 2ch, 1sc into next ch, rep from * endi⟨ with 1dc into last ch. Turn.

2nd row. *Ch2, 1sc into space before 3dc group of previous row, ch⟨ 3dc into 3rd dc of previous row, rep from * ending with 1dc i⟨ space between last sc and turning ch. Turn.

The 2nd row forms pattern and is repeated throughout.

Chainmail stitch
Make a number of chains divisible by 2, plus 1.

1st row. Into 2nd ch from hook work 1sc, 1sc into each ch to en⟨ Turn.

2nd row. Ch3, skip first sc, *insert hook in next st, yoh, draw ya⟨ through, yoh, draw through first loop on hook, yoh, draw throu⟨ first loop on hook, yoh, draw through 2 loops on hook, ch1, sk⟨ 1sc, rep from *, ending with 1dc into last st. Turn.

3rd row. Ch2, work 2sc into each space of previous row to end. Tur⟨
Rows 2 and 3 form pattern and are repeated throughout.

Using these stitches for a stole
Any of these attractive, intricate stitches can be used to make ⟨ elegant fringed stole.

Begin and end with two rows of doubles and allow for five ex⟨ doubles at each end of the rows to give a border effect. Wh⟨ completed, trim the short edges with two rows of scallops ⟨ working four chains, skipping one double, then working one sin⟨ crochet into the next double and adding a fringe to the ne⟨ scalloped row.

Fan stitch
Chainmail stitch

▲ *Lattice stitch*
▼ *A pretty fringed stole crocheted in lacy jasmine stitch (see Crochet Know-how chapter 20, p. 386)*

▲*Triangle stitch*

Crazy stitch

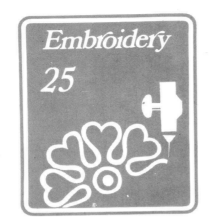

Embroidery 25

Embroidery by machine

In recent years, embroidery designers have become more fully aware of the tremendous design potential of machine embroidery—not only for adding an individual touch to clothes and household linen, but also for creating unusual pictures and wall hangings.

Whether you have an up-to-date deluxe zigzag machine or are still using your grandmother's old treadle, you can produce beautiful effects and patterns yourself. In this chapter and the following machine embroidery chapters, Creative Hands describes the techniques and uses of this exciting and rewarding twentieth-century craft. The sampler illustrated opposite shows that even an ordinary home sewing machine can work wonders!

The main advantage of machine embroidery over hand embroidery is the obvious one of speed. Then, how much you can achieve is related to the level of sophistication of your machine; for example, although it is possible to do some machine embroidery using a fairly old-fashioned machine, there will be limits.

There are three types of machine embroidery: straight stitching with the foot on the machine, using varying threads for decorative effects; free-motion embroidery with the foot off the machine; zigzag pattern embroidery. (Interesting effects can be achieved using the straight-stitch method by winding thicker thread onto the spool.)

Free-motion embroidery

For free-motion embroidery, the presser foot of the machine is removed and the teeth which feed the material under the needle lowered. Once this has been done, the fabric itself can be moved in every direction, while the machine is running.

Uses of machine embroidery

The adaptability of machine embroidery is, of course, similar to that of hand embroidery. It helps to make clothes look more individual, adds interest to household items like towels and tablecloths, or becomes an art form if used for making appliqué pictures. Once you have followed the machine embroidery chapters and mastered the basic technique, you will then be able to experiment and work out new and original ideas.

What your machine can do

The old treadle machine was foot operated, strong and could be relied upon to do a running line of stitching on almost any fabric, however thick. It was used for dressmaking and household sewing. There are very few treadles left, but if you have one, it is possible, with the machine foot still in place, to do several simple, thicker stitches with thicker than normal threads in the spool. With the foot off, you will be able to experiment with a basic running stitch

of varying thicknesses and with different tensions.

The hand-operated models came next and these were smaller, portable and more convenient except that they were only straight-stitch machines and slow to work, as they left only one hand free to guide the fabric. Hand-operated machines are usually only to be found in museums today.

The simple electric model enabled the operator to use both hands to guide the fabric and to sew faster in a straight stitch.

Again, with the foot on, this machine will work simple stitches in thicker yarns. Once you have taken off the foot, you will be able to experiment with yarns, stitch sizes and tension variations.

The electric zigzag machine which was introduced after World War II was more versatile. This machine made zigzag as well as straight stitches available to the public and made it easier to sew a stitch with a width as well as a length.

With the foot still on this model you can experiment with thicker stitches, zigzag and satin stitches. On some models there is a shuttle design for twin needles to work tucking, appliqué, eyelet holes and hemstitching. In free-motion embroidery you will have a choice of basic running stitch plus zigzag stitch and variations.

Deluxe zigzag machines with built-in patterns set in motion with the flick of a lever or turn of a dial were the next advance.

There are obvious advantages in having this kind of machine to do embroidery. With the foot still on the machine you can try thicker stitches plus zigzag and satin stitch patterns, using the twin needle for double patterns and tucking, appliqué, eyelet holes and hemstitching. In free-motion embroidery the basic running stitch plus the zigzag stitch can be used.

Free arm machines are not very suitable for machine embroidery unless they adapt to an ordinary flat-bed style.

Preparing to work

Needles for machine embroidery

With machine embroidery, needles should be carefully selected because the eye will have to accommodate a thread which normally might not be used with the particular fabric.

As with straightforward sewing, care should be taken with the choice of needle used in the machine. A thin fabric requires a thin needle, for example, No.11 American or 70 Continental, and fine thread. A medium fabric requires a No.11 or 14 American needle, 80 Continental and medium thread. A thick fabric should be worked with a No.16 American needle or 90 Continental and slightly thicker thread.

Threads for machine embroidery

Embroidery and decorative stitches can be worked in machine embroidery cotton No. 50 or No. 30 as well as in varying thicknesses of normal sewing thread. Since these are generally imported, they are hard to find. Thicker embroidery threads can be wound onto the spool.

Stitch length and tension

Experiment with altering tensions and length of stitch. In most cases tensions must be adjusted for the top thread and are marked numbers on a disk or indicated by a plus or minus sign. Spool cases have either one or two screws. When there are two, the one on the left is a set screw which holds the tension bar in place and the one on the right is the tension screw. When the spool case has only one screw, then that is the tension screw.

Turn the tension screw clockwise with a small screwdriver to tighten the thread and anti-clockwise to loosen it. Embroidery generally requires a tension slightly looser than normal.

The stitch length, if adjustable, is usually indicated by a number dial or lever.

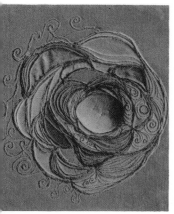

Machine embroidery, raised areas
Hand-winding a spool

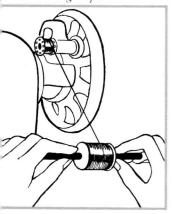

Machine embroidery on velvet
Machine with the foot off

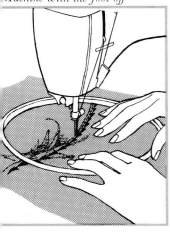

Treadle and simple electric
1. *Stitching with loose tension, thick yarn in spool*
2. *Vermicelli effect in a free pattern using a small stitch*
3-6. *Straight stitch with a thick yarn in the spool*
7. *Free pattern in straight stitch, hand applied beads*
8-13. *Different yarns on the spool*
14. *Applied ribbons using a straight stitch down each edge*
15-20. *As for rows 8-13*

Zigzag machine
21. *Satin stitch*
22. *Pattern built up using varying widths of satin stitch which are linked with lines of straight stitching using a thicker thread in the spool*
23. *Satin stitch*
24-28. *Satin stitch and zigzag worked in varying widths, spacings and tensions*
29. *Satin stitch worked in varying widths by moving the stitch width lever by hand*
30. *Decoration worked in free embroidery using zigzag stitch. Hand-sewed beads*
31. *A simple geometric pattern worked around felt diamonds and decorated with square wooden beads. The second row out from the diamonds is a length of wool couched to the fabric with a small zigzag stitch*
32. *Narrow tuck stitched with two rows of straight machine stitching, one row simple, the other using a thicker yarn in the spool and a loose spool tension*
33. *A deeper tuck stitched with a wide satin stitch and a thick yarn on the spool*

Deluxe zigzag machine
34 & 35. *Programmed patterns*
36 & 37. *Satin stitch holding narrow velvet ribbon in place*
38 & 39. *Programmed patterns*
40. *As for 33*
41. *As for 32*
42-48. *Variations of tucking. Rows 42 and 48 are decorated with glass beads sewed on by hand*

(N.B. The numbers identify the row)

Dragons in embroidery

Rearing its ferocious head, the dragon has always been a popular motif in traditional embroideries. With its long twisting tail, scaly body and nostrils exhaling fire, the dragon is a particularly decorative monster whose shape lends itself well to a design.

The dragon (below) on this page is one of the many exotic animals which adorn a bed hanging, made by Abigail Pett, and now on display in the Victoria and Albert Museum in London, England.

Each curtain of the bed hanging is designed with six or seven motifs, showing mythical landscapes with trees, flowers and animals. The dragon is one of the larger motifs, and has been worked in bold stitches. Solid areas of embroidery are sewn in long and short or split stitch, graduating from dark to light in definite stripes.

On other parts of the curtain, flower petals, leaves and hills are textured, made from various patterns such as laid or couched work, cross-stitch, satin, feather and herringbone stitch.

The Syon cope (opposite) depicts a two-headed monster, half-dragon, half-serpent, which has been slain by the virtuous Saint Michael (Victoria and Albert Museum). Originally made as a vestment in the thirteenth to fourteenth century, this beautiful embroidery was later converted to a cope, or long ecclesiastical cloak. The subdued coloring is achieved by the use of colored silks and gold threads, worked in couching and fine split stitch. Couching worked on the underside of the material makes a chevron pattern on the upper surface.

A winged dragon displays savage characteristics as it grapples with a leopard. This magnificent tapestry (left) is at the Wawel Castello, Cracovia, in Poland.

Bobbin Lace 1

The grace of lace

In the great lace-making cities of the world tourists can watch women making lace with impressive skill. Of course, we could never hope to achieve what has taken a lifetime's dedication to learn. But lacemaking can be an absorbing and fascinating hobby and with plenty of patience and practice you should be able to achieve ambitious results.

Making lace with bobbins is a craft with very ancient origins. In the areas where lace is still made, the craft has been handed down through the generations for hundreds of years. No one is absolutely certain where bobbin lace, or pillow lace as it is sometimes called, was first made. The earliest traces of its history date from around the fifteenth century, but experts still argue as to whether it was the Italians or the nuns of the Benedictine Order of Cluny in France who were the first bobbin lacemakers.

The traditional patterns are still practiced today, but Creative Hands plans to bring you new design ideas, such as ways to use thick gold threads and large bobbins to make sumptuous hangings, sleeves and collars.

The lace is made by intertwining a specific number of threads previously wound onto bobbins. There is no doubt about the fact that lacemaking is difficult at first, so you must be prepared for a lot of patient practice until you have mastered the basic stages and can work them automatically. It is well worth persevering, though, since there are very few more fascinating and beautiful crafts.

Lacemaking materials

- [ ] Bobbins
- [ ] Lace pillow
- [ ] Thread
- [ ] Lacemakers' pins
- [ ] Pricking card
- [ ] Punch or pricker point holder and points

Bobbins. The bobbin is a wooden rod with a small head at one end. Some bobbins have beads threaded on the end to weight them. The thread is wound around the bobbin so that it acts as a spool and also weights the thread so that it can be more easily manipulated.

It is still possible to come across lace bobbins, often made of ivory, in antique or junk shops. Because of their rarity they can be expensive, but you might be lucky enough to find some quite cheaply. Generally speaking, old bobbins are far more ornamental than new ones.

Lace pillow. The lace pillow is used as a base on which to work the lace and is usually cylindrical, about 14 inches long and 7 inches in diameter, although this can vary. The pillow should be very heavy and is usually filled with straw or sand. The shape of the pillow is, however, purely a matter of tradition—in Bruges lace for example, square pillows are used.

If you want to make your own lace pillow, choose a light-colored covering because it is less tiring on the eyes when working. A very fine linen or cotton is a good choice of fabric, but if you plan to fill the pillow with straw, burlap is just as suitable.

Special stands for lace pillows can be bought, but you can just as easily use heavy books instead. The important thing to remember is that the pillow must be kept firmly in place while the lace is being worked.

Thread. Lacemaking thread does not necessarily have to be very fine—some modern laces are quite heavy with a bold look. Whatever the thickness of the thread, it must be strong and twisted.

Pins. Lace pins are used to hold patterns in shape until they are completed. They should be fine and long and made of metal which does not rust. Brass pins or brass-plated ones are best.

Pricking card. The pricking card is used to trace the lace pattern and can be bought by the sheet. A pattern is marked out on the card and worked over it.

Pricker. The pricker, or punch, is used to make holes in the card pattern where the pins will be placed.

How to begin

Perfect lace depends on having a good chart and on making certain it is firmly fixed to the pillow to prevent it from sliding around. the circumference of the pillow is smaller than the length of the chart, add some padding between the pillow and the chart so that the ends of the chart meet. If you buy a ready-made chart, you will find that the patterns are marked with consecutive numbers at points where the thread passes. This makes things much simpler, so it is best to use a purchased chart when you are a beginner.

Winding the bobbins

1. Wind the thread around the narrowest part of the bobbin. Holding the bobbin in the right hand, arrange the end of the thread in a double loop by winding it twice around the first two fingers the left hand.

2. Insert the head of the bobbin into the loop.

3. Hold the loop in place with the index finger of the right hand and pull the end of the thread with the left hand.

4. Continue to ease the thread through until the knot is in place.

The number of bobbins used varies according to the lace being made, but it is always an even number. Not all the bobbins are used at the same time and when there are a great many, those not being used are pinned to one side or tied together to keep them out of the way.

The length of thread between the bobbins and the lace should be about six inches, otherwise the threads can become tangled.

These are the tools of lacemaking and the basic method of preparing them. You can now progress to learning the basic steps of the bobbin movements which are described in detail in the next Bobbin Lace chapter. Practice the movements until they become comfortable and automatic. Continued working of these basic movements produces an attractive braid which will make a trimming for cloth or household items, depending on your choice of thread. In addition Bobbin Lace chapter 2, page 514, shows you how to work a basic background—a slightly different technique, worked to a pattern in the same way as with more complex laces.

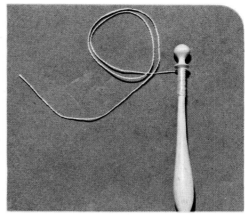

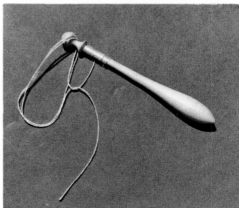

▲ *Wind thread on bobbin and loop end twice*
▼ *Insert head of bobbin into loop*

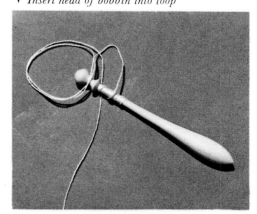

▲ *Gently pull the thread end*
▼ *Gradually ease the knot into place*

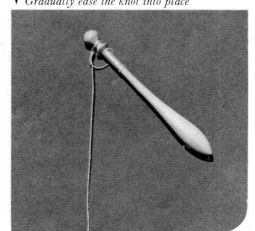

▲ *Lacemaking still thrives in many places. Here you see the famous Maltese lace being made*
▼ *A bobbin lace pattern being worked on a pillow supported on a stand*

Making unlined draperies

Draperies can work magic in the home—bringing a touch of brilliant color to rooms which are dark or diffusing the harsh light of others. Problem windows can have their problems solved, or a room can be given a special character, with imaginative use of fabrics and window fittings. This chapter shows how to plan and make unlined draperies.

Working with sheers and nets

As these fabrics come in generous widths, there is no need for widths to be seamed together. Selvages are usually neat on these fabrics and side hems are unnecessary, but all stitching should be finished off with a reverse stitch to prevent the stitches from coming undone. Use a special lightweight heading tape for gathering.

▼ *The modern look: unlined, translucent semi-sheer draperies*

What you need to know

How to measure for drapery track

Before buying drapery fabric, install drapery track or traverse rods on all windows to be covered. Not only will your draperies look more professional hung from the track, but they will wear better too. Curtain rods are not satisfactory (except possibly for nets, although even these look more elegant on a track).

Drapery tracks should extend the width of the window plus 6 inches at each end, so that the drapes can be drawn back to give maximum daylight. If the drapes are to overlap in the center, two sections instead of one continuous piece are required, and 4 extra inches should be allowed on the length of each section. Traverse rods with built-in opening and closing features and stops at each end can be bought in various sizes and can be expanded or contracted to the desired length.

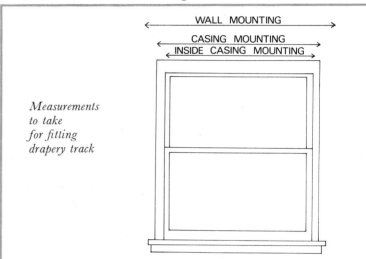

Measurements to take for fitting drapery track

Types of drapery tapes and hooks

The gathering and pleating of draperies is made easier by using the gathering tapes available in the stores. There are several different types available—some produce a soft gather, others deep formal pleats. The tape which produces soft gathers is designed to gather approximately a double width of material. The more formal pleating tapes gather as much as three times the fullness of material. Drapery hooks are available for all types of tape and are very similar in design and application. Most drapery tracks have their own range of hooks.

Suitable fabrics for unlined draperies

Unlined draperies show to best advantage with light filtering through them—good fabrics for this are coarsely woven linen and synthetic semi-sheers. Some of the brilliantly patterned fabric look even better with the light behind them, but it may be necessary to have a second, lightweight drapery close to the window if privacy at night is necessary. Drapery fabrics usually measure between 48 and 50 inches wide, while sheers and nets from 36 inches wide up to 120 inches wide are available.

How much fabric to buy

Measuring the amount of drapery material you require need not worry you. It is a matter of simple mathematics. First, measure the width of fabric needed. Measure the length of the drapery track and multiply by two (for double fullness). To this, add a sum of inches for an allowance for side hems, usually 2 inches on each side of each drape. Add a further 6 inches to each width if the drapes are to overlap in the center. The total is the width o fabric needed for the *pair* of drapes. For windows measuring more than 4 feet wide, it is necessary to join widths of material to achieve the overall width necessary for gathering. The chart shows the number of widths you will need for different sized windows.

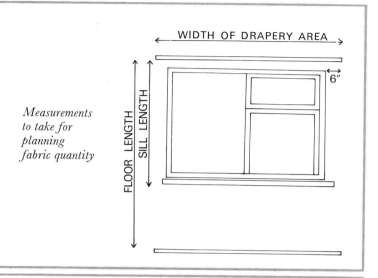

Measurements to take for planning fabric quantity

Widths of fabric required

Width of drapery area	Number of widths required per drape (for simple gathered head)
4′ 6″ and under	1
4′ 6″—5′ 6″	1½
5′ 6″—7′ 6″	1½
7′ 6″—10′ 0″	2

How to measure for length

Using a steel tape measure or a yardstick, measure the length from the drapery track to either the window sill or the floor (see diagram). To this measurement add 6 inches for a double 3 inch hem at the bottom and add 2½ inches for the heading.

This measurement, multiplied by the number of widths required, will give you the length of material required for a pair of drapes. If you choose a pattern with a large repeat, extra fabric will have to be allowed for matching. Widths seamed together must match as to pattern and all the windows in the room must match. Although the salesman may be able to help you when you choose your fabric, for a general rule of thumb you will need an extra pattern repeat on each drapery length: e.g. (see diagram) for three drapery widths, allow three extra pattern repeats.

Allow extra fabric for matching large patterns

Making the draperies

Cutting and seaming

Place the fabric on a large, flat surface for cutting—the floor is ideal if you don't have a large table. Make one end absolutely straight by drawing a thread and cutting along the line. Measure and mark with pins for the first width. Fold the material along the line marked with pins and cut along the fold. Match the pattern if necessary, and cut off the second width in the same way. Continue until all the widths are cut.

If it is necessary to cut half a width, for draperies taking half widths for instance, fold a width lengthwise, and cut along the fold. Cut the selvages off both edges and join the widths (and half widths), using a flat-fell seam. Use a loose tension and a long stitch for stitching the seams.

Stitching unlined draperies

Unlined draperies require a good hem at the sides to prevent them from curling back. Fold over 1 inch and then another inch, pin and baste and then stitch the side hems or hand sew, using a loose blanket stitch (the stitches should be about ¼ inch apart).

Turn up 3 inches and then another 3 inches on the bottom hem and sew by hand, using a loose blanket stitch.

Turn the top edge of the drape over 2½ inches and make a basting line 1½ inches down from the folded edge. Cut a strip of gathering tape the width of the drape plus 2 inches for turnings. Pull out the cords from the part of the tape to be turned under and pin and baste the gathering tape to the drape along the line of basting. Turn under the ends of the tape and baste along the bottom edge of the tape. If you are stitching the tape to the drape, stitch both edges in the same direction to prevent any drag in the stitching which would show on the finished drape.

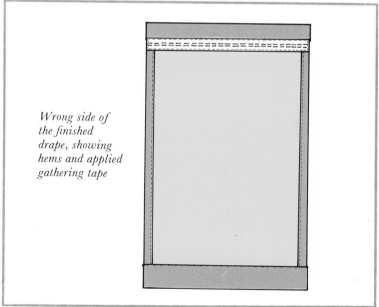

Wrong side of the finished drape, showing hems and applied gathering tape

Gathering draperies

Secure the cords at each end of the tape by knotting them together or stitching them securely. Draw the cords up from the middle of the tape and ease the fabric so that it is evenly gathered and the correct width for the window. Knot the cords in the middle and catch them to the tape with one or two little stitches to prevent the knot from hanging down.

The advantage of gathering from the middle is that the gathers are easily released by cutting these little stitches and undoing the knot when the draperies need cleaning or laundering.

A great little dress

Here's a dress to delight a small member of the family. It's a basic pattern, shown here made up in hard-wearing cotton corduroy and trimmed with a sparkling white collar, which is detachable for easy cleaning. This little dress is given in three sizes, to fit a 24, 26, and 28 inch chest. The patterns are on graph and each dress consists of three pattern pieces only. It's quick and easy to do and yet it's versatile enough for you to be able to make a whole wardrobe of excitingly different little dresses for all sorts of occasions from this one pattern. Try it and see!

Dressmaking for children can be easy and fun

You can make this dress in different types of fabric with various trimmings, and here are some ideas to get you started.

For play, make it in hard-wearing cotton or corduroy and add big patch pockets. For parties, as a complete contrast, make it in something light and filmy. Choose plain or embroidered organdy, organza or voile for a top dress, then stitch it to an underdress in matching or contrasting cotton lawn or taffeta. For a really delicate look, trim it with lace or add frills.

For vacations and beach wear, make a sleeveless version in terry cloth and, to make it really practical, stitch a row of apron pockets across the front to hold all those pretty pebbles and shells gathered on the beach.

There are some washable wools available for making cozy and practical winter dresses, and you can add detachable collars and cuffs to change the appearance of each dress quickly. You'll see how to make these in the next Dressmaking chapter, page 516.

The basic pattern

The patterns on the graph are in three sizes: 24in chest, length 22½in; 26in chest, length 24in; 28in chest, length 26½in. Each square represents a 1 inch square.

To copy the pattern, use graph paper or any firm paper drawn accurately into 1 inch squares. Before you begin, select the pattern size you want and cut the paper into pieces just large enough to accommodate each pattern graph. Then copy the outline of the pattern to scale.

It is easy to adjust the length of the pattern by adding to or deducting from the squares between the lower edge of the armhole and the hemline. Do not add or deduct at the hem, because the flare of the dress will be affected, as with the flared skirt pattern. If you need to cater to in-between sizes, select the larger of the two sizes and pin off the difference at the fitting stage.

Making fitting easier

Small children often get very fidgety if they have to stand still to be fitted, and sometimes a fitting session can end in tears and bad temper. You may only have an hour or two during the school

Key to graphs for the child's basic dress

The patterns are in three sizes
24in chest, length 22½in
26in chest, length 24in
28in chest, length 26½in
Each square on the graph represents a 1 inch square
The patterns do not include seam allowances

Color key to sizes
Size 24in chest = ————
Size 26in chest = ————
Size 28in chest = ————

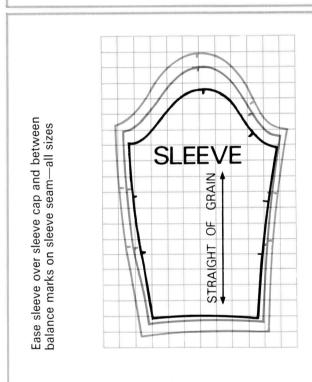

Ease sleeve over sleeve cap and between balance marks on sleeve seam—all sizes

SLEEVE

STRAIGHT OF GRAIN

day when you can get down to some dressmaking, and it may be difficult to get beyond the fitting stage.

One way to help you over these problems is to make a mock dress for the child (this is not quite the same as a muslin—it's not necessary to make a muslin for a child—but to be successful, children's dresses do need careful fitting).

Make it from sheeting or muslin as for the blouse bodice muslin. (It's a good idea to cut out a miniature dress for the child's doll at the same time. The child can copy all the fitting stages and it will keep her busy too while you do your work.)

Cut out the mock dress as if it were the real one with ¾ inch seam and 2½ to 3 inch hem allowance. Pin and baste the front and back together along the side and shoulder seams. Leave the center back seam open so that it is easy to slip on and off. Put the mock dress on the child and pin it together down the center back.

The first fitting

With most children, there are four special fitting points—dropped shoulders, chubby neck, chubby arms and a high tummy. All these points affect the fitting of a dress.

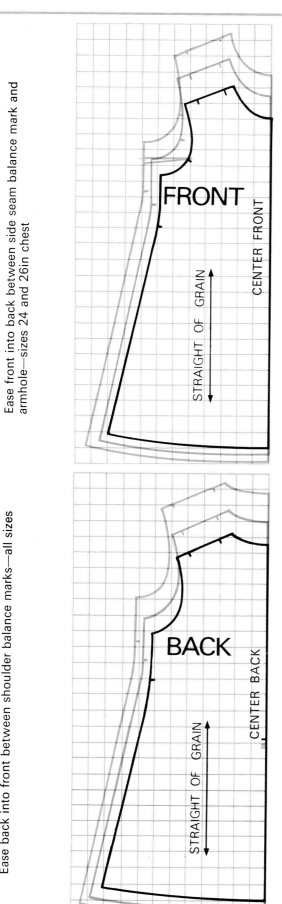

Ease front into back between side seam balance mark and armhole—sizes 24 and 26in chest

FRONT

STRAIGHT OF GRAIN

CENTER FRONT

Ease back into front between shoulder balance marks—all sizes

BACK

STRAIGHT OF GRAIN

CENTER BACK

Dropped shoulders. Pin off the required amount from the outer edge of the shoulder seam. Snip the seam allowance around the lower armhole until the creases running toward the underarm have disappeared, both back and front. Mark a new underarm seamline with pins or pencil if necessary.

Chubby neck and arms. Snip the seam allowance around the neck and armholes until the dress lies flat. Mark the new seamlines.

A high tummy. If the dress juts out in front, make a side bust dart as shown on the pattern for size 28 inch chest. If you are using this size already, lift a little more fabric into the dart. In either case, the amount you take into the dart must be added to the hemline at the side of the dress, otherwise the hem allowance will be reduced.

The child with a high tummy often stands very erect, a posture which will make the dress appear rather tight across the chest and full across the back. If you can avoid it, do not alter the width across the back because this is needed for movement—add width across the front instead. This means making a new front pattern, but this is not difficult.

To make a new front pattern, lay the pattern piece on a large sheet of paper, pinning the center front to one straight edge. Measure 4 inches from the edge and slash the pattern from the hem to within $\frac{1}{8}$ inch of the shoulder. Spread the left half of the pattern piece until the opening at chest level is about $\frac{1}{2}$ inch wide. If this results in too much flare at the lower side seam, trim the flare as shown in diagram 1. Straighten the shoulder line and cut out the new pattern.

The second fitting

Make the mock dress just as if it were the real one, except for the neckline. Trim off the seam allowance along the seamline to fit perfectly around the neck. Put in the sleeves to give you the correct setting for them and turn up all hems.

Try the dress on the child again. When you are satisfied that it fits, cut the dress into sections along the stitching lines. Place the sections flat, over the pattern pieces, and transfer all the alterations. Having done this, your problems are solved because you can use the pattern again and again with only a brief check on the fitting now and then.

Hems

Little dresses are often made with hems up to 6 inches deep, but it is a mistake to think that a child's dress will last longer if it is made with a really deep hem. The truth is that this adds a great deal of weight to the garment and can make it look quite shapeless. Bear in mind, too, that when a dress becomes too short for a growing child, it affects not only the hem but also the length between shoulder and underarm and this, in turn, makes the sleeves too tight. Of course it may be possible to alter the dress, but it is rather a waste of time to go to this trouble if the dress is only going to be worn once or twice before the seams split. Making a dress "on the big side" is not the answer either, because the sad result would be a new dress which is shapeless turning into a dress which fits only when it is worn out! The answer is to make a dress which fits well right from the start, then the child can enjoy wearing it and you can be proud of having made it. A hem of 3 to 4 inches, if you want to allow extra, is adequate and will give the dress a good life of two or three seasons.

Neckline finishes

Another important point to watch when making children's dresses is the neckline finish. This section is rubbed a great deal during washing and it has to withstand a lot of wear, so a good, firm finish is necessary.

To hold the neckline in shape, make a rouleau-type bound

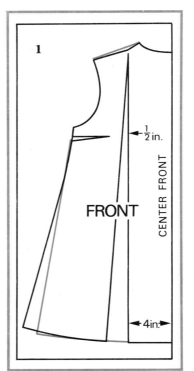

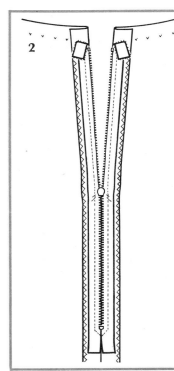

1. *Making a new front pattern* **2.** *Zipper tape ends sewn in place*
▼ *Detail of the finished neckline, bound with a bias strip*

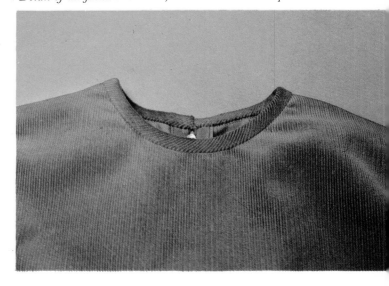

finish (described under making instructions). Apart from being very hard-wearing, it looks neat and will also withstand the repeated stitching which is necessary when changing detachable collars for washing.

A flat bias facing is an alternate finish but does not give such a strong neck edge. This is because the seam allowance inside the bias must be snipped close to the seam to lie flat.

It is not advisable to use conventional fabric facings for children's dresses, because they become worn and very untidy after frequent washing.

Fabric requirements for the child's dress

36in wide fabric. Twice the dress length plus the sleeve length and hem and seam allowances.

54in wide fabric. The dress length plus the sleeve length and hem and seam allowances.

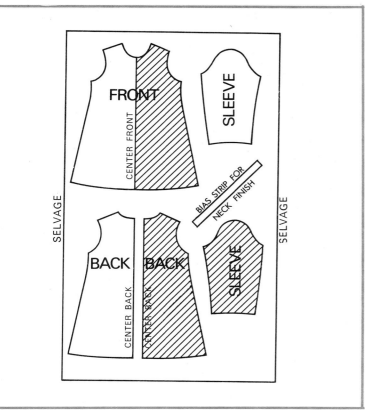

Layout for the child's dress on 36in width, with or without one way
Layout for a child's dress on 54in width, with or without one way

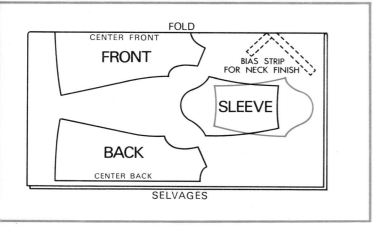

You will also need a zipper (12in for size 24in chest, 14in to 16in for sizes 26in and 28in chest, depending on the dress length), and one size 1 hook for the neck fastening.

If you want to be really economical when calculating the fabric length, make a trial layout on paper first, using the same methods as for the child's skirt and vest in Dressmaking chapter 23, page 454. You can then measure the yardage from your own layout and buy the exact amount of fabric.

If you decide to add pockets or frills, don't forget to take this into account when working out the yardage.

The layout
Copy one of the layouts illustrated or use the layout you made on paper to calculate the yardage.

On your own layout, place the center front of the pattern on the fold and the center back on the selvages, allowing for a center

back seam. Make sure that the grain line marked on the sleeve pattern piece lines up perfectly with the grain of the fabric.

Pin all pattern pieces down securely and mark around them. Mark all pattern details, not forgetting the end of the zipper opening. Cut out the dress, adding seam and hem allowances.

Making the dress

This basic dress is so simple that you can make it in six easy stages. It's easier still if you have made and fitted a mock dress first.

1. Seams and darts
Pin, baste and stitch the small side bust darts (if you need to use them) and press them toward the hem.

Pin, baste and stitch the side and shoulder seams and the center back seam below the zipper opening. Finish all seam edges neatly and press the seams open.

2. The zipper
Stitch in the zipper as for a straight seam, leaving 1 inch between the zipper teeth and the raw edge of the neckline. Turn back the ends of the zipper tape at an angle so they will not show and hand-sew them down, as shown in diagram 2.

3. The sleeves
Pin, baste and stitch the sleeve seams, finish the seam edges neatly and press the seams open. Gather in the ease around the sleeve caps and pin the sleeves into the armholes, matching balance marks and seams. Stitch, remembering to work with the sleeve uppermost. Finish seam edges and press the seams into the sleeves.

4. Binding the neckline
First, to hold the shape of the neck edge and to prevent it from stretching, machine a row of stay stitches along the seamline. Trim off the seam allowance $\frac{1}{8}$ inch from the stay stitches.

To bind the neck, cut a bias strip from the dress fabric (or an equally strong contrasting fabric) $1\frac{1}{8}$ inches wide and $\frac{1}{2}$ inch longer than the neck edge measurement.

Pin and baste the bias strip to the neckline on the outside of the dress, right sides facing and raw edges even, leaving $\frac{1}{4}$ inch at each end for turning. Stitch in position, taking $\frac{1}{4}$ inch seam allowance to bring the stitching line for the binding $\frac{1}{8}$ inch below the stay stitching. Do not trim any more fabric off the seam allowance as this is now your guide for the width of the binding.

Turn in the $\frac{1}{4}$ inch seam allowance at each end of the bias strip and turn under the raw edge. The amount you turn under depends on the thickness of the fabric you are using, but the folded edge should meet the stitching line when turned to the inside of the dress.

Never force the bias strip over the neck edge or it will pucker. If the bias strip is tight, let out the folded edge a little until the bias strip can be turned over the raw edge without strain. Slip stitch the folded edge to the stitching line and close the ends of the binding. Finish with a hand-made bar and hook.

5. Making the hems
Turn up the hem allowance on the dress and the sleeves. Make the hem in the usual way on the dress, but on the sleeves use a firmer hemming stitch. Sleeve hems are easily caught by little fingers in a hurry to get dressed.

6. The finishing touches
Press the dress and all seams and hems on the inside, being as careful as you are with your own dresses. This final touch is not only necessary but also justifies all your dressmaking efforts.

Fashion Flair

A bunch of gay ribbons

Ribbons have long been a fashion favorite because of their romantic appeal. Use them to brighten any garment.

1. *Lace up the shoulders of a crêpe evening dress with ribbons threaded through brass rings, the ends flowing free.*
2. *A ribbon fringe, each ribbon end finished with a feather, adds interest to a plain dress.*
3. *Make rosebuds of ribbon to decorate a sweetheart neckline.*
4. *A basket weave of wide satin ribbon makes for unusual sleeves.*
5. *Satin ribbons tied around the waist of a jersey dress give texture contrast.*
6. *Ribbon kisses covering a dress and down its sleeves. Thread narrow ribbon through the holes in cobweb woven fabric.*

Creative Hint. To make ribbon basket-weave sleeves, cut out the sleeve shape in fabric. Plan a grid on the shape and mark with lines of basting, keeping to the straight of the fabric. Lay strips of ribbon edge-to-edge across the sleeve, cutting each piece of ribbon to the correct sleeve width. Pin and baste, and then machine stitch each ribbon strip along both ends. Now weave strips of ribbon in and out of the horizontal ribbons along the length of the sleeve. Pin and baste, then machine stitch down both ends of the ribbon. Cut excess ribbon away and stitch the sleeve seams in the usual way.

Cross-stitch tulips

Pattern Library

These bright, crisp tulips have a certain charm and character in their simplicity of design. Whether embroidered on fine linen or on a coarse-weave fabric, this is a design which you will find endlessly useful.

It makes a pretty border for a little girl's dress. Partly because of its childlike quality, it almost has a toy-town appeal and is what you might expect a tiny girl to turn out for a first, rather shaky, attempt! Borders like this are also ideal for towels and other household items. Use the motif singly on a pocket, dotted around in an all-over pattern for a pillow or tablecloth, or to border a child's bedspread.

Make a perfect "V"-line

A well-knitted garment can be spoiled by a badly finished "V"-neck which doesn't lie flat. The variations here will help you achieve a professional-looking neckline every time.

These neckbands are worked on two needles, allowing for a seam at the center back of the neck. They can also be added to a garment by picking up stitches around the neck, but again, two needles must be used and one shoulder left unseamed so that the neckband can be worked in rows. For an even more attractive finish on the single rib examples shown here, cast on and bind off using invisible method (see Knitting Know-how 2, pg. 8, and 6, pg. 102). Count the number of rows on the right and left fronts from the center "V" point and allow one stitch for every row and one stitch for every stitch of the back neck bound-off stitches. Note the multiples of stitches, plus extra stitches, which are required to keep the rib correct on either side of the center point. For example, the double rib neckband requires two center stitches and multiples of four stitches plus two extra stitches.

Single rib neckband with center shaping using slip stitch decreasing

Cast on the required number of stitches, noting that the center stitch must be a purl stitch for the right side of the work. Mark the center stitch with colored thread.

1st row (right side). Work in K1, P1 rib to within one st of center st ending with K1, sl next st and center st P-wise, P next st and pass 2 slipped sts over this st, beg with K1, work in rib to end.

2nd row. Rib to one st before center st, sl next st and center st K-wise, P next st and pass 2 slipped sts over this st, beg with K1, work in rib to end.

Rep these 2 rows for required depth of neckband. Bind off in rib, still decreasing at center point, or bind off invisibly.

Single rib neckband with center shaping combining two methods of decreasing

Cast on the required number of stitches, noting that the center stitch must be a knit stitch for the right side of the work. Mark the center stitch with colored thread.

1st row (right side). Work in K1, P1 rib to within one st of center st ending with P1, sl the next st K-wise, K center st and next st tog, psso, beg with P1, work in rib to end.

2nd row. Rib to one st before center st, P next 3 sts tog, beg with P1, work in rib to end.

Rep these 2 rows for required depth of neckband. Bind off in rib, still decreasing at center point, or bind off invisibly.

Single rib neckband with center stitch using slip stitch decreasing

Cast on the required number of stitches, noting that the center stitch must be a knit stitch for the right side of the work. Mark the

▲ *Single rib neckband with center shaping using slip stitch decreasing method*

▲ *Single rib neckband with center shaping combining two methods of decreasing*

center stitch with colored thread.

1st row (right side). Work in K1, P1 rib to within 2 sts of center st ending with P1, K next 2 sts tog tbl, K center st, K next 2 sts tog, beg with P1, work in rib to end.

2nd row. Rib to 2 sts before center st, P2 tog, P center st, P2 tog, beg with P1, work in rib to end.

Rep these 2 rows for required depth of neckband. Bind off in rib, still decreasing at center point, or bind off invisibly.

Single rib neckband with center stitch combining two methods of decreasing

Cast on the required number of stitches, noting that the center stitch must be a knit stitch for the right side of the work. Mark the center stitch with colored thread.

1st row (right side). Work in K1, P1 rib to within 2 sts of center st ending with P1, sl 1, K1, psso, K center st, K2 tog, beg with P1, work in rib to end.

2nd row. Rib to 2 sts before center st, sl 1, K1, psso, P center st, K2 tog, beg with P1, work in rib to end.

▲ *Single rib neckband with center stitch combining two methods of decreasing*

▲ *Double rib neckband with two center stitches combining two methods of decreasing*

▼ *An example of a single rib neckband, the "V"-neck stitches picked-up and bound-off by the invisible method*

Single rib neckband with center stitch using slip stitch decreasing method

...ep these 2 rows for required depth of neckband. Bind off in rib, ...ill decreasing at center point, or bind off invisibly.

...ouble rib neckband with two center stitches combining ...o methods of decreasing

...ast on the required number of stitches, noting that the two center ...tches must be knit stitches for the right side of the work. Mark ...e two center stitches with colored thread.

...t row (*right side*). Work in K2, P2 rib to within one st of center 2 ...ending P2, K tog next st and first of 2 center sts, sl second center ...K next st, psso, beg with P2, work in rib to end.

...d row. Rib to one st before 2 center sts, P next st and replace it ...left-hand needle, sl first of 2 center sts over this st and re-...ace st on right-hand needle, P tog second center st and next st, rib ...end.

...d row. Rib to one st before 2 center sts, K tog next st and first of 2 ...nter sts, sl second center st, K next st, psso, rib to end.

...ep 2nd and 3rd rows for required depth of neckband. Bind off ... rib, still decreasing at center point.

Town and about coat

This slim and elegant town coat is warm enough for early spring yet, being unlined, is light enough to be indispensable to your summer wardrobe. The skirt and bodice are worked in an easy patterned stitch with simple doubles used for the yoke, sleeves, collar and pocket.

Although the photograph shows the coat worked in green crepe yarn with white trim, you can, of course, choose any color or colors you like. Directions for crocheting buttons are in Crochet Know-how chapter 28, pg. 546 or chapter 8, pg. 146.

Sizes

Directions are for 32in bust with 34in hips.
The figures in brackets [] refer to the 34, 36 and 38in bust sizes with 36, 38 and 40in hips.
Length from shoulder, 34½ [35: 35½: 36]in.
Sleeve seam, 17in adjustable.

> **Gauge**
> 8 doubles and 5 rows to 2 inches worked on No.F crochet hook.

Materials

Unger Cruise
8[9:10:11] 1-4/10 oz. balls in main color A
1 ball in contrast color B
One No. F (4.00 mm) crochet hook
One No. G (4.50mm) crochet hook
Seven buttons

Back

Using No.F crochet hook and A, ch98[102:106:110].
504

Base row Skip 2ch, work 1dc into each ch to end. Ch3 to turn. 97[101:105:109]dc.
Work 1 row dc.
Continue in patt:
1st row (right side) Using No.F crochet hook, work in dc to end. Ch2 to turn.
2nd row Using No.G crochet hook, work in sc to end. Ch2 to turn.
3rd row *Skip 1sc, 1dc into each of next 3sc, put hook in front of last 3dc and into skipped sc, yoh, draw through long loop, yoh, draw through 2 loops on hook, rep from * to last st, 1sc into last st. Ch1 to turn.
4th row Work 1sc into each st to end. Ch2 to turn.
Rep 3rd and 4th rows once more.
7th row Using No.F crochet hook, work 1dc into each st to end. Ch2 to turn.
Rep 7th row 4 times more, ending last row with ch1 to turn.
Rows 2-11 form patt.
Rep rows 2-11 once more.**
Rep 2-11 patt rows 5 times more, dec 8sts evenly across the first row of 1st, 3rd and 5th patt rep. 73[77:81:85]sts.
Rep 2-11 patt rows twice more, inc 4sts evenly across the first row of 1st and 2nd patt rep. 81[85:89:93]sts.
Continue working each row in dc only until work measures 26in from beg or required length to underarm, ending with a WS row. Skip turning ch at end of last row.

Shape armholes

Next row Ss over 9[10:11:12]
sts, work in dc to last 9[10:11:

12] sts. Ch2 to turn. 63[65:67:69] sts.
Continue without shaping until armholes measure 8[8½:9:9½]in, ending with a WS row.

Shape shoulders

Next row Ss over 6[6:7:7] sts, work in dc to last 6[6:7:7] sts. Turn. Rep last row once more.
Next row Ss over 7[7:6:6] sts, work in dc to last 7 [7:6:6] sts.
Fasten off.

Right front

Using No.F crochet hook and A, ch50[54:58:62].
Work as given for back to **. 49[53:57:61] sts.
Rep 2-11 patt rows 5 times more, dec 4sts evenly across the first row of 1st, 3rd and 5th patt rep. 37[41:45:49] sts.
Rep 2-11 patt rows twice more, inc 4sts evenly across the first row of 1st patt rep. 41[45:49:53] sts.
1st and 2nd sizes only
Work 1 row dc, inc 3[1] sts across the row. 44[46] sts.
3rd and 4th sizes only
Work 1 row dc, dec 1[3] sts across the row. 48[50] sts.
All sizes
Continue working in dc until work measures same as back to underarm, ending at armhole edge.

Shape armhole

Next row Ss over 9[10:11:12] sts, work in dc to end. 35[36: 37:38] sts.
Continue without shaping until armhole measures 5 rows less than back to shoulder, ending at armhole edge.

Shape neck

Next row Work in dc to last 10sts. Turn.
Continue in dc, dec one st at neck edge on next 4 rows.

Shape shoulder

Next row Dec one st, work in dc to last 6[6:7:7] sts. Turn.
Next row Ss over 6[6:7:7] sts, work in dc to last 2sts, dec one st.
Fasten off.

Left front

Work as given for right front, reversing all shapings.

Sleeves (two alike)

Using No.F crochet hook and A, ch35[37:41:41].
Work base row as given for back, then work in dc for 2in. Continue in dc, inc one st at each end of next and every other row until there are 70[72:76:76]sts.
Continue without shaping until work measures 17in from beg, or required length to underarm. Place colored marker at each end of last row. Work 2in more for cap of sleeve, which is set into armhole. Fasten off.

Collar

Join shoulder seams.
Using No.F crochet hook and A and with WS of work facing, work in dc over center 8sts of back neck, ss over all sts to end of back neck. Ch3 to turn. Work in dc over all sts of back neck, work in dc

Sparkling white on shamrock green ►
▼ *Pattern stitch and pocket detail*

over 7sts of left front neck.
Ch3 to turn.
Work in dc to right shoulder,
work in dc over 7sts of right
front neck. Ch3 to turn.
Continue working in dc across
all neck sts, inc one st at each
end of every other row; *at
the same time* inc 4sts evenly
across every other row 3 times.
Fasten off.

Pocket flaps (2 alike)

Using No.F crochet hook
and A, ch12.
Work 5 rows dc.
Fasten off.

Attach yarn to side edge and
work 1 row dc around 3 sides
of pocket, working 2sts in
each corner st. Break off A
and attach B. Work 1 row dc
as before.
Fasten off.

Finishing

Press all pieces lightly on WS
under a damp cloth with a
warm iron. Sew side seams.
Sew sleeve seams as far as
markers. Sew in sleeves, sewing
cap of sleeves from markers
to bound-off sts at underarms.

Edging

Using No.F crochet hook
and A and with RS facing,
attach yarn to lower edge of
right front and work 1 row
dc along right front edge,
working 7 buttonholes evenly
spaced by skipping the length
of the button required and
working ch3, the first
buttonhole to come 9in from
lower edge and the last 8in
below neck shaping; continue
in dc around revers and collar
working twice into corners sts,
and down left front. Break
off A. Attach B and with RS
facing beg at side seam and
work 1 row dc evenly all
round edges of coat, working
twice into corner sts.
Fasten off.
Using No.F crochet hook
and B, work 1 row dc around
cuffs.
Fasten off.
Press all seams. Sew on
pocket flaps and buttons.

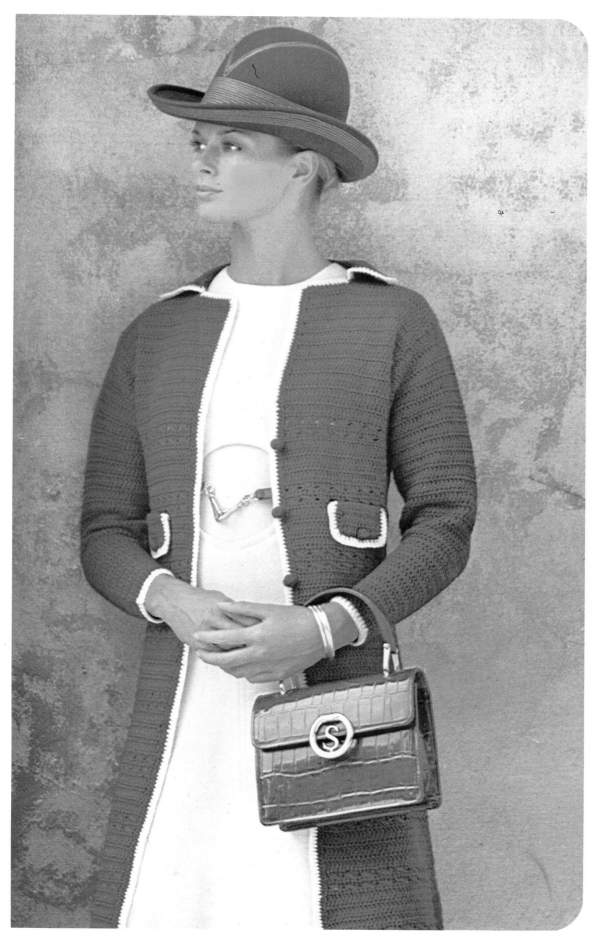

The fabric feel of crochet

These very firm, fabric-like stitches can be used for garments which receive a lot of wear—suits, jackets, skirts, coats and dresses, for instance. When you are working these stitches, choose a plain, untextured kind of yarn rather than anything fancy or the fabric effect will tend to become lost. You will find that the close, compact nature of the stitches uses yarn very quickly, so allow a little extra when you are working out a garment pattern.

When you have completed all the stitch swatches, they could be stitched together to make a colorful pillow cover. If you make each square 4 inches by 4 inches and allow 9 squares for the front and the back of the pillow, you will arrive at a pillow measuring 12 inches square. Three of each pattern in different, vividly contrasting colors would make a completely original and individual furnishing accessory.

Double single crochet

Make a chain of the desired length.

1st row. Insert hook into 3rd ch from hook, draw yarn through, yoh, draw through 1 loop, yoh, draw through 2 loops on hook to form 1 double single crochet, work 1 double single crochet into each ch to end. Turn.

This row forms the pattern and is repeated throughout by inserting the hook into each st of the previous row and beginning each row with ch2 as the turning ch.

Up and down stitch

Make a number of chains divisible by 2, plus 1.
1st row. Into 3rd ch from hook work 1sc, *1dc into next ch, 1sc into next ch, rep from * to end. Turn.
2nd row. Ch2, *1sc into dc, 1dc into sc, rep from * to last st, 1sc into last st. Turn.
The 2nd row forms the pattern and is repeated throughout.

Double up and down stitch

Make a number of chains divisible by 4, plus 1.
1st row. Into 3rd ch from hook work 1sc, 1dc into each of next 2ch, *1sc into each of next 2ch, 1dc into each of next 2ch, rep from * to end. Turn.
2nd row. Ch2, 1sc into 2nd dc, *1dc into each of next 2sc, 1sc into each of next 2dc, rep from * to last 2sts, 1dc into each of last 2sc. Turn.
The 2nd row forms the pattern and is repeated throughout.

▲ *Double single crochet*

Raised basket weave stitch

Make a number of chains divisible by 4, plus 3.
1st row. Into 2nd ch from hook work 1sc, 1sc into each ch to end. Turn.
2nd row. Ch2, 1sc into each sc to end. Turn.
3rd row. Ch2, work 1sc into each of next 2sc working into the back loop only of the row below, *work 1sc into next sc inserting the hook into the corresponding st on the row below the previous row and drawing up a long loop, work 1sc into each of next 3sc working into back loop only of the row below, rep from * to end. Turn.
4th row. As 2nd.
5th row. Ch2, *work 1sc into next sc inserting the hook in the corresponding st on the row below the previous row and drawing up a long loop, work 1sc into each of next 3sc working into back loop only of the row below, rep from * to last 2sts, work 1sc into next sc inserting hook and drawing up a loop as before, 1sc into back loop only of last sc. Turn.
Rows 2-5 form the pattern and are repeated throughout.

Leaf stitch

Make a number of chains divisible by 2, plus 1.
1st row. Into 3rd ch from hook work 2sc, skip 1ch, *2sc into next ch, skip 1ch, rep from * to last st, 2sc into last st. Turn.
2nd row. Ch2, *skip 1sc, work 2sc into 2nd sc of group, rep from * to end. Turn.
The 2nd row forms the pattern and is repeated throughout.

Little leaf stitch

Make a number of chains divisible by 2, plus 1.
1st row. Into 3rd ch from hook work 1sc, ch1, 1sc into same st, skip 1ch, *1sc, ch1, 1sc into next st, skip 1ch, rep from * to last st, 1sc, ch1, 1sc into last st. Turn.
2nd row. Ch2, *into ch between 2sc of previous row work 1sc, ch1, 1sc, rep from * to end. Turn.
The 2nd row forms the pattern and is repeated throughout.

Up and down stitch
Double up and down stitch

▲ *Raised basket weave stitch*
▼ *Leaf stitch*

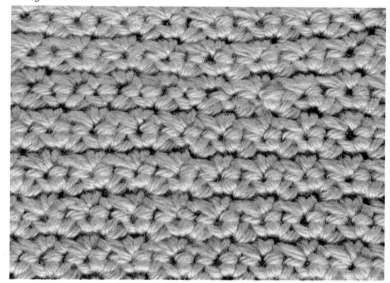

▼ *Little leaf stitch*

Straight stitch and programmed patterns

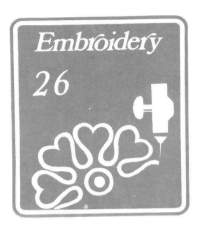

Embroidery 26

This chapter deals with decoration and embroidery worked with the presser foot on the machine and the use of programmed patterns. The effects are different from free-motion embroidery which is worked with the presser foot removed and the feed teeth lowered. (This type of embroidery is described in detail in the previous embroidery chapter, p. 488.

The machine is used in the same way as for dressmaking, but sometimes threads, tensions and needles differ according to the desired result.

Decoration of this kind can be applied to clothes and accessories, and to household items such as pillow covers, curtains and pictures or wall hangings. Stitches worked with the foot on the machine are neat and practical, lie flat on the surface of the fabric and are easily washed and cleaned.

Both the pretty dresses illustrated are decorated using techniques described in this chapter.

Designing

Long straight lines or simple curves are better than short lines, because if the lines of the design are not continuous, the ends of the thread will have to be darned through to the back of the work.

Applying design to fabric

Guide lines of the design, which have to be followed by the machine needle, can be marked on the fabric with dressmaker's chalk. (Never use a pencil on the right side unless it has a very soft lead and then use it lightly, otherwise the lead will mark both the fabric and the thread.)

Sometimes it is possible to trace the design onto thin paper such as tracing paper or onionskin. Baste this onto the back of the work and stitch or baste the main guide lines from the back. Turn the work to the right side to stitch the embroidery.

N.B. Hard, unpliable, closely woven fabrics with a shiny finish are difficult to use as they pucker badly.

Method of embroidery

For all work stitched with the foot on the machine (except eyelet holes and tucking), the fabric is placed on thin paper. This paper prevents puckering, especially when the zigzag or satin stitch is used. The paper does not have to be basted to the fabric and is pulled away after all the embroidery is completed.

Thicker threads

No.30 sewing cotton is used on top of the machine and the work is stitched on the wrong side. Paper is still used on the back of the work and the design guide lines can be drawn on it.

Thicker threads, such as pearl cotton No.5 and No.8, 6-strand

floss and thin wool, are wound onto the bobbin by hand. The tension screw in the bobbin case is loosened or completely removed so that the thread runs very loosely. The top tension should be reasonably tight. This technique can be used on a straight-stitch machine or a zigzag machine. The length of stitch should be adjusted and also the width of stitch on a zigzag machine to get varied results.

Metallic threads

When using metallic threads it is not possible to wind the thread onto the bobbin on the machine in the usual way. This kind of thread is so brittle that running it through all the thread guides would only damage or snap it. Instead, slot a pencil through the spool and feed it directly from this to the bobbin winder. Keep the thread untwisted if it is a flat-sided lurex thread (see Embroidery 25, p. 488). The bobbin tension must be loose and the top tension fairly tight so that only the metallic thread shows on the right side of the work. This technique is worked face downward and can be used on straight-stitch and zigzag machines and for the patterns on deluxe zigzag machines. Fine metallic threads are now available which can be worked from the top with a slightly looser top tension.

Stitches, patterns and techniques

Zigzag, satin stitch and deluxe zigzag patterns

Machine embroidery cotton No.30 and sewing cottons are used for these stitches. The bobbin and top of the machine are threaded with the same kind of thread.

Experiment by altering the length and width of the zigzag stitch—when the zigzag stitch is closed up, it becomes satin stitch. The zigzag stitch and satin stitch should look smooth with the stitches locked together at the back of the work, which means a slightly looser top tension than bottom tension. If the tension is too tight the embroidery will not lie smoothly and the fabric will pucker. The deluxe zigzag patterns can look very effective when worked with double needles and different colored threads. This kind of work is always embroidered right-side up.

Hemstitching, tucking and eyelet holes

Hemstitching can be worked with single or double hemstitching needles. Embroidery cotton is used and this form of decoration usually done on organdy or organza.

Tucking is worked with twin needles and a matching pin tucking foot. These come in different widths. Some machines insert cord automatically as you sew, making the tucks broader and more durable. Backing paper is not used for this decoration, since the two threads have to be pulled together by the bottom thread to make raised tuck. Although this technique is based on the simple straight stitch, it can be achieved only on a zigzag or deluxe zigzag machine with twin needles.

Eyelet holes

These may require a special eyelet embroidery plate and foot. Pierce a hole in the fabric with an embroidery stiletto and then place the fabric in an embroidery hoop. The feed is lowered so that the hoop can be swung freely around in a circle to make the satin stitch around the hole.

All these fascinating techniques are quick to do, which is the main advantage of machine embroidery. They are easy to learn, but some machines differ from others, any extra information can be found in the instruction booklet of your particular machine. you bought one secondhand without a manual, the manufacturers are usually able to supply one.

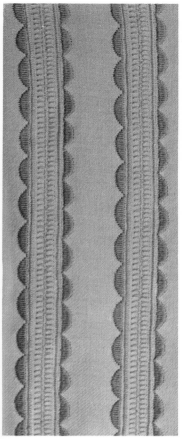

Stitch detail of pale dress
Automatic patterns—instant charm ▶
Stitch detail of pink/gray dress

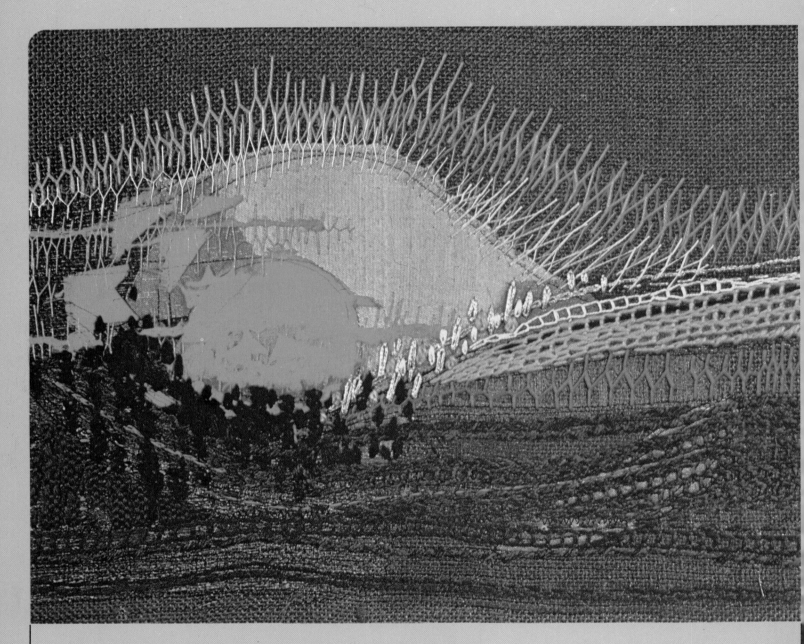

Collector's Piece

The Red Sun

The designer of this unusual example of abstract embroidery
was inspired to reproduce, in fabric, the effects of dazzling sun
on a landscape. The foreground depicts undulating hills and
plowed fields, lit up in places by the sun's brilliant rays in
the background. Contrasts in tone and texture were created by
careful choice of stitches and threads, producing
interesting effects of light and glowing color.
Two main types of stitch have been used for this piece of work.
The sun has been sewn in cretan stitch, worked upright in
blocks, while the stitches above the sun, also in cretan, are
slanted to give the effect of movement. The rest of the
embroidery has been worked in chain stitch; in the foreground,
single chain stitches of gold and navy give the impression of

dappled light and shade produced by the sun.
The landscape of hills and plowed fields was achieved by
lines of open and twisted chain stitch. Vertical lines of raised
chain band in dark brown and navy counteract the horizontal
flow of the other chain stitches, making the sun a focal point.
This imaginative stitching is enhanced by contrasting areas of
plain fabric, and by the use of shot fabrics which lend a glow
to the entire work. A feeling of vitality and movement is given
to the embroidery by the effect of light on the cretan stitches.
Throughout the composition, all the stitches and threads, the
textures and colors of the fabrics, have been selected carefully
for their individual characteristics.
Valerie Tulloch designed and worked this embroidery.

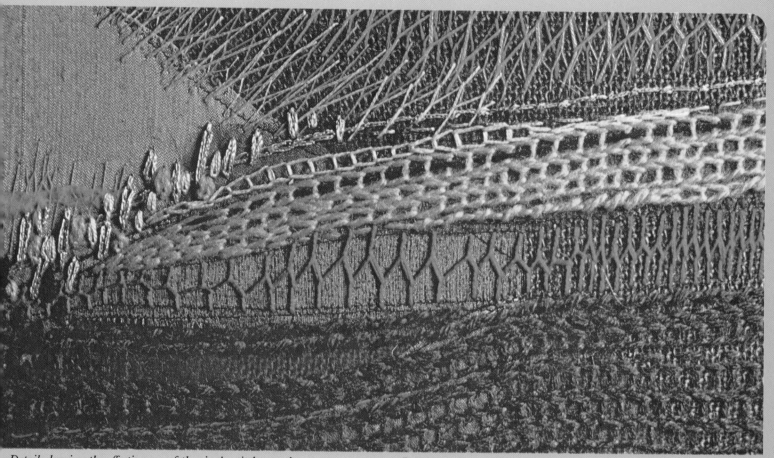

Detail showing the effectiveness of the single stitches used

▼ *The sun's brilliance is accentuated by dappled shade in the foreground*

Cushioned with flowers

These gay bunches of summer flowers embroidered in tent stitch are just the thing to scatter all over a cushion, or to make a series of little pictures for a bedroom. Use one of the individual motifs to make a lovely decoration for a pincushion, needlecase or purse.

The motifs are shown worked in tent stitch but could look interesting worked in cross-stitch. Or you could try working a textured background stitch to add more interest. Worked on a very fine canvas, with 22 single threads to 1 inch, the motifs would make charming brooches or pendants, or even a set of large buttons.

▲ *Pretty ideas using flower motifs*

Materials you will need

For a pillow 16in by 16in
☐ ¾yd 26in wide double-thread canvas, 10 double threads to 1in
☐ ½yd backing material (dress tweed or upholstery fabric)
☐ Foam pillow form 17in by 17in
☐ D.M.C. Tapestry yarn

Suggested color scheme
Pansy motif—
☐ purple 7243 ☐ violet 7709
☐ yellow 7742 ☐ brown 7506
☐ black   ☐ green 7911
Pansy background—
☐ beige 7520, pale turquoise 7956 or pale yellow 7745
Nosegay motif—
☐ green 7911 ☐ orange 7946
☐ tangerine 7947 ☐ cream 7726 ☐ yellow 7742
Nosegay background—
as for pansy.
Rose motif—
☐ pink 7202 and 7205 ☐ green 7387 and 7402 ☐ brown 7506 and 7499 ☐ yellow 7742
Rose background—
☐ beige 7520 or green 7361

Main section
Cut a piece of canvas measuring 19in by 19in. Mark down the center with a row of cross-stitches and then mark th crosswise center row in th same way.

Mark off the canvas into six teen squares of 40 by 40 doubl threads with similar rows o cross-stitch.

These dividing rows can b worked in oblong cross-stitc in a slightly darker tone of th background color or in on of the colors of the design.

Work a flower motif in eac square using tent stitch, mal ing sure the flower is in th center of its square.

Backing
Cut a piece of material 17¼i by 17¼in.

To make the pillow
Block the needlepoint (fc this see Needlepoint chapt 5, page 112). Trim the canva leaving ⅝in turnings.

Fold the turnings to the bac of the work and baste, miterir the corners.

Turn in the backing sea allowance, baste and press. P the backing to the front c three sides, carefully matchir corners. Baste and whip t three sides.

Insert the pillow form ar whip the remaining side.

▼ *The nosegay motif*

▼ *Chart for nosegay motif*

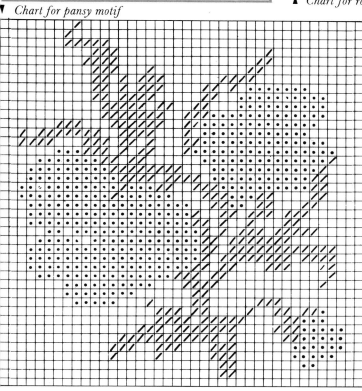

▲ *Richly decorated pillows for a touch of luxury*

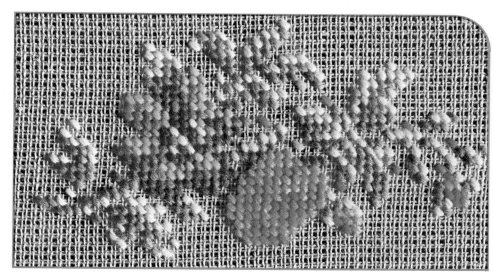

▲ *The rose motif*

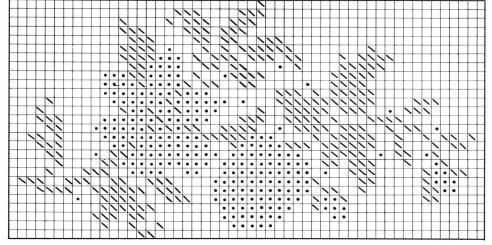

▲ *Chart for rose motif*

▼ *Chart for pansy motif*

▼ *The pansy motif*

513

'Bobbin' along in lace

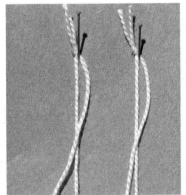

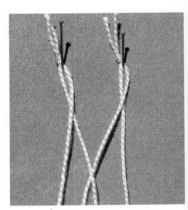

▲ *Stage one: turning*　　　　▲ *Stage two: crossing*

Once you have the necessary equipment described in Bobbin lace chapter 1, page 492, the next step is to become familiar with the basic stitches which go into the formation of lace. This chapter shows you the basic bobbin movements and some basic foundation stitches. Practice these until you have mastered them sufficiently to do them comfortably and automatically. Don't be discouraged if you find the technique difficult at first. Lacemaking is an art and requires a great deal of patience but is a most rewarding craft. The next chapter gives instructions for mesh foundations which, although only basic backgrounds, are pretty in themselves.

Bobbin movements

For basic lacemaking, a set of four bobbins is required, one pair for each hand. Tie the four threads in pairs, making sure the knot is secure. Fix the threads to the lace pillow with lace pins, either between the threads or through the knot itself. Fix the threads to a chart at this stage.
The following are the basic lacemaking movements. Practice them until they become automatic, carefully following the instructions and illustrations when you begin.

Turning
This term describes the movement of passing the right bobbin over the left one.

Crossing
When there are four bobbins, cross the inside bobbin of the left pair over the inside bobbin of the right pair. The outside bobbins are not moved.

Half stitch
Turn both pairs of threads and then cross the center threads. Fix the half stitch in place with a pin.

Full stitch
This is made by working a turning and a crossing immediately followed by another turning and crossing. The left pair of bobbins has now been transferred to the right side and the right pair to the left side.

Braid
A close braid is made by working several full stitches consecutively.

Herringbone background
Work this background on four bobbins. Using the fourth bobbin, turn with the third bobbin, cross with the second, turn with the first one and pin. Still using the fourth thread, turn with the first bobbin, cross with the second, turn with the third and pin. In this way the fourth bobbin is passed from right to left and back again in a zigzag, weaving between the first three threads.

Weave foundation stitch

This is a basic stitch which is used to make the main motifs of lace patterns. Nearly all weave stitches are made horizontally, with the exception of some more complex stitches which are worked diagonally.
Copy the chart onto a piece of cardboard or lacemaking parchment and pin it firmly to the lace pillow.
Place 3 pairs of bobbins to point **a**, 2 pairs to point **b** and 2 pairs to point **c**.
*Cross the first 2 pairs of bobbins as if each pair were one thread. Then, using the same 4 bobbins, make a half stitch. Cross the 2nd and 3rd pairs and make a half stitch. Cross the 3rd and 4th pairs and make a half stitch. Cross the 4th and 5th pairs and make a half stitch. Cross the 5th and 6th pairs and make a half stitch. Cross the 6th and 7th pairs and make a half stitch. Place a pin at point **1** on the chart and place the last pair of bobbins there. Turn this pair of bobbins and start working back. Cross the 7th and 6th pairs and make a half stitch. Cross the 6th and 5th pairs and make a half stitch. Cross the 5th and 4th pairs and make a half stitch. Cross the 4th and 3rd pairs and make a half stitch. Cross the 3rd and 2nd pairs and make a half stitch. Cross the 2nd and 1st pairs and make a half stitch. Fix the 1st pair of bobbins on a pin at point **2** on the chart, then turn them. Repeat from *.

Filet work foundation stitch

For square pieces of lace, borders and festoons, this stitch makes up the main motifs of the pattern. The motifs are linked by an open-work background.
Copy the chart onto a piece of cardboard or lacemaking parchment and pin it securely to the pillow.
Fix a pair of bobbins to each of the points **a**, **b**, **c**, **d**, **e**.
Turn the 1st and 2nd pairs of bobbins and cross.
*Turn the 2nd and 3rd pairs and cross, repeat with the 3rd and 4th pairs and then with the 4th and 5th pairs.
Turn the 5th pair of bobbins out at the right of the work and fix with a pin at point **1** on the chart.
Turn the 5th pair of bobbins twice and the 4th pair once and cross.
Turn the 4th and 3rd pairs and cross, repeat with the 3rd and 2nd pairs and then the 2nd and 1st.
Fix the crossing with a pin at point **2** on the chart. Turn the 1st pair of bobbins twice, 2nd pair once, and cross. Repeat from *.

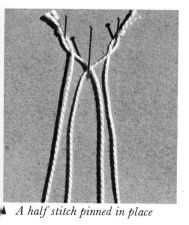
▲ A half stitch pinned in place

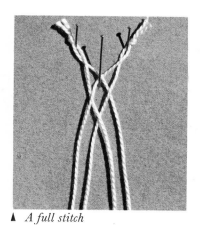
▲ A full stitch

▲ Full stitches forming a braid

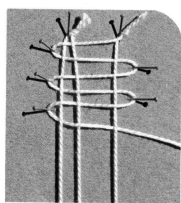
▲ Herringbone background

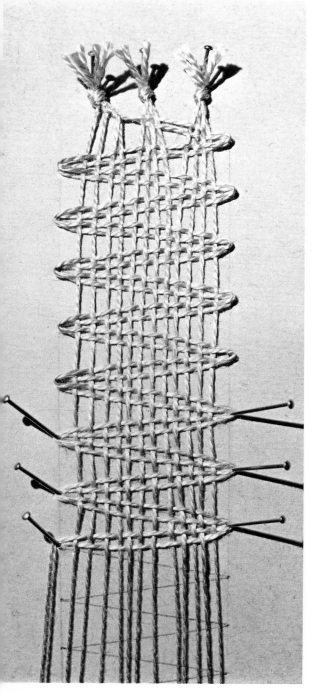

◄ Weave foundation

▼ The pattern chart

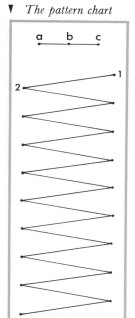

Filet foundation stitch ►

▼ The pattern chart

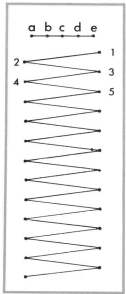

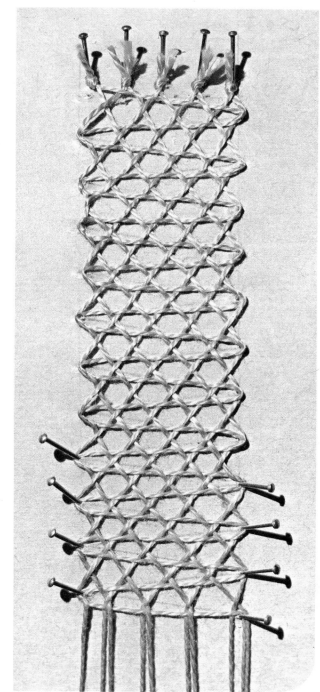

Dress-making 26

Collars and cuffs

This chapter includes tracing patterns for Peter Pan, puritan and yoke collars, and also a simple cuff. They are designed for the girl's basic dress in Dressmaking 25, page 496, but the patterns can be adjusted for use in any simple dress.

Collars

Suitable fabrics for making collars

Cotton piqué is a traditional fabric for making trimmings such as collars, and it is the most useful. It is very hard wearing, and collars made in this fabric will always look crisp and retain their shape even after frequent washing.

For really pretty collars you can use organdy or lace, but collars made in these fabrics will naturally be quite delicate and require more careful handling.

Collar making does not end with plain collar shapes—there are many ways you can trim them using braid, lace edgings or embroidery. A very pretty idea is to embroider a realistic little butterfly on one side of the collar to look as though it has just settled there.

Fabrics requirements and notions

You will need:
- □ ¼yd 36in wide fabric for the Peter Pan collar
- □ ⅜yd 36in wide fabric for each of the puritan and yoke collars
- □ One package of soft cotton bias binding

The collar pattern sizes

These patterns will fit a dress neck opening of 15¼ inches.

Trace the collar patterns, using the instructions given on page 518. Cut out the patterns.

To make any of the patterns larger, cut along the two dash lines and lay the sections on a sheet of paper. Divide the extra collar length required by four and spread each cut section by this amount. Pencil around the new outline and cut out the new pattern.

To make a pattern smaller, divide the amount by which the collar is to be shortened by four and fold off this amount along both dash lines. Lay the altered pattern on a sheet of paper; pencil around the new outline and cut out the new pattern.

Cutting out the collars

You will need four collar pieces to make the Peter Pan and puritan collars and two pieces for the yoke collar.

Fold the fabric, following the layouts given on page 518. Be very careful to lay the patterns on the correct grain of the fabric; otherwise, when the collar is stitched in place, it will not lie well around the neck of the dress. The center front of the yoke pattern is placed on the fold as shown. Cut out, allowing ⅜ inch seam allowance on all edges.

Making the collars

All the collars are made in the same way, except that the Peter Pan and puritan collars are made in two sections and the yoke collar in one.

Lay two corresponding collar pieces together, right sides facing. Pin, baste and stitch around the outer edges, leaving the neck edge open.

Trim the seam allowance to ¼ inch and trim across the corners to remove the bulk. If necessary, make "V" notches around the front curves on the Peter Pan collar so that the seam allowance inside the collar will lie flat when the collar has been turned. Do not notch the seam allowance on the puritan or yoke collars because the notches will show as dents from the outside.

Turn the collar sections to the right side, baste the stitched edges and press.

On the Peter Pan and puritan collars overlap the seam allowance at the center front and hold together with a catch stitch as shown in the diagram opposite.

Stitch the collar along the neck edge, snip into the seam allowance, and finish the raw edge with bias binding.

Press the collar. Then press the bound edge to the underside of the collar, ready to sew in position on the dress. As you press the binding under the neck edge, stretch it so that it follows the shape of the collar.

Attach it to the dress with long slip stitches.

Using organdy and lace

Organdy. If you use this fabric, make the collars as described in the previous paragraphs, but trim the seam allowance to 3/16 inch or, if the organdy is particularly firmly woven, to ⅛ inch. This is because the seam allowance will be visible through the fabric.

Lace. Some patterned lace is constructed in such a way that you can use the pattern to form a pretty edge simply by cutting around the outline. If the outline of the lace pattern is corded, as with guipure lace, and you can avoid cutting through this outline when cutting out the collar, you need not finish the outer edge any further. But if the lace is liable to fray, use a fine whip stitch (see Dressmaking 21, p. 416) over the pattern outline to secure the edge and finish the raw neck edge with bias bindings as before. If the lace you are using does not allow you to cut in this manner cut the shape for a top collar from the lace and an under collar from organdy or organza. This will highlight the pattern of the lace and you can stitch the collar as if you were using plain fabric.

Trimming the collars

A little lace edging can turn an ordinary collar into a party-goer. For washable collars use cotton lace which will stand up to handling and ironing.

Most fine cotton lace edgings can be gathered or pleated without being bulky. Just be sure to ease in sufficient fullness to allow the outer edge of the lace to remain nice and full too. Nothing looks worse than lace gathered on the inside of the curve and flat on the outer edge.

To make sure that you buy enough trimming, measure along the edge of the collar and buy at least twice this amount. If the lace is very fine, much of it will disappear in the gathers, so you'll need two-and-a-half times the length of the edge of the collar.

Guipure daisy and fine ball fringe edging are especially pretty. These cannot be gathered, so you simply stitch them to the outer edge, on top of the collar. Just remember to ease the trimming to follow the roundness of the edge, otherwise it will turn up and over during wear.

You can give a really decorative look to an organdy collar for a rich velvet dress by using either double-edged lace, which is drawn up through the center to make a double frill, or a fine slotted lace

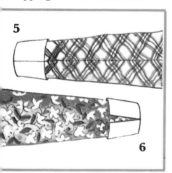

Peter Pan **2.** Puritan **3.** Yoke

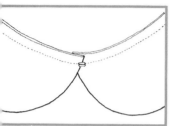

...verlapping the seam allowance

Tube-shaped cuff **6.** Pointed cuff ▲ The child's basic dress trimmed with lace cuffs and Peter Pan collar

...ith ribbon slotted through the center. Buy extra ribbon and you
...n make tiny bows to sew along the lace at intervals.
...he lace collar, too, will look even more lacy if you trim the edge
...ith matching lace edging.

...uffs

...ffs are another pretty form of trimming, either used on their own
... made to match a collar. They can also be put to good practical
...e to lengthen sleeves which have become too short.

... point to remember when using cuffs as a trimming: Sleeves
...ould be shortened ½ inch because the roll of the cuffs will add
... the sleeve length.

...ffs are easy to make and just as interchangeable as collars.
...ou can use the same list of suitable fabrics, too.

...bric required: For the cuff pattern given here, you will need
... yard of 36 inch wide fabric.

...e pattern: Trace the pattern from the outline on page 518.
...ngthen or shorten as necessary, using the instructions given for
...e collars, but dividing by two instead of four.

...tting: Lay the pattern on the correct grain and cut four pieces
...vo for each cuff), allowing ⅜ inch seam allowance all around.

...vo ways to stitch the cuffs

...be-shaped cuffs. Stitch the ends of each of the four sections to
...ke four tubes. Then, with right sides facing, pin, baste and stitch

two matching sections together along the upper, wider, edge. Trim
the seam allowance, turn to the right side, edge-baste and press.
Stitch along the lower raw edges of each cuff and finish with bias
binding.

Pointed cuffs. With right sides facing, pin, baste and stitch two
matching sections along the sides and upper, wider, edges. Trim
the seam allowance, turn to the right side, edge-baste and press.
Stitch the lower raw edges together and finish with bias binding.
You can trim the cuffs using the methods given for collars.

Attaching the cuffs

For both types of cuff, attach the narrower edge of the cuff to the
sleeve. Using long slip stitches, sew the cuff to the inside of the
sleeve, ½ inch from the hem.

Position the tube-shaped cuff with the cuff seam corresponding
with the sleeve seam, and the pointed cuff with the open end
opposite the sleeve seam.

Roll up the cuff over the edge of the sleeve and make small catch
stitches under each one where it meets the sleeve seam. With
pointed cuffs, sew each point down invisibly. This will prevent
the cuffs from rolling down.

Self cuffs

You can also use the cuff pattern to make cuffs from self fabric and
attach them to the sleeves permanently.

Simply stitch the lower raw edge of each cuff to the seam allowance
of the sleeve, turn both edges under and face with a bias strip.

517

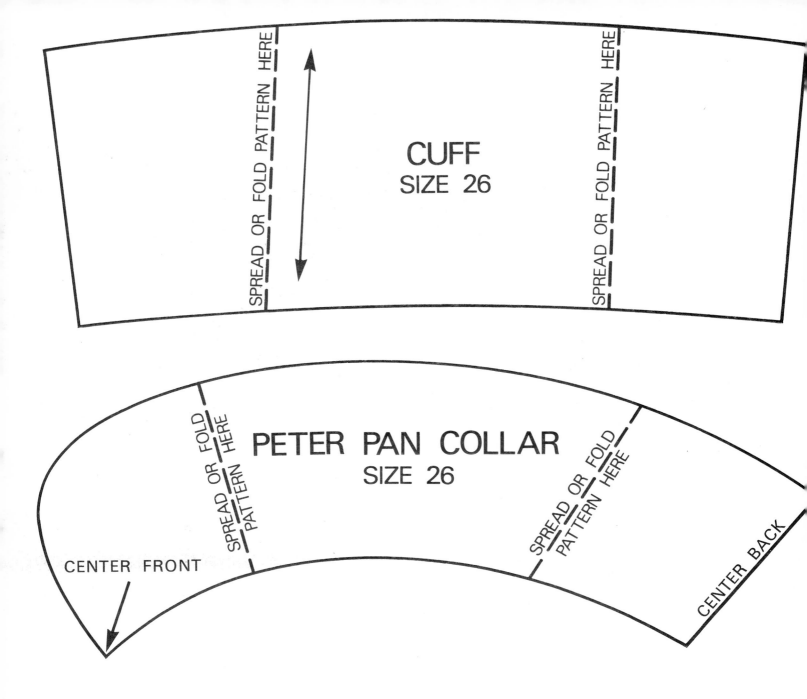

CUFF
SIZE 26

SPREAD OR FOLD PATTERN HERE

SPREAD OR FOLD PATTERN HERE

PETER PAN COLLAR
SIZE 26

SPREAD OR FOLD PATTERN HERE

SPREAD OR FOLD PATTERN HERE

CENTER FRONT

CENTER BACK

The patterns

The tracing patterns given here are for three collar shapes and one cuff shape, designed for the child's basic dress in Dressmaking chapter 25, page 496. All the patterns fit the dress size 26in chest with a neck opening of 15¼ inches. No seam allowances are given.

The dash lines on the patterns indicate where to lengthen or shorten them.

The straight of grain for the Peter Pan and puritan collars is the straight edge along the center back. The straight of grain for the yoke collar is the fold edge of the center front. The straight of grain for the cuff is indicated on the pattern.

Layout for the Peter Pan collar on 36in wide fabric without one way

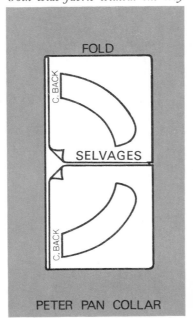

FOLD

C. BACK

SELVAGES

C. BACK

PETER PAN COLLAR

Layout for the puritan collar on 36in wide fabric without one way

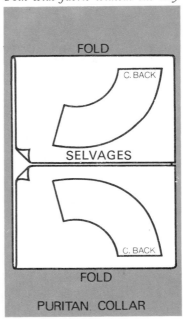

FOLD

C. BACK

SELVAGES

C. BACK

FOLD

PURITAN COLLAR

Layout for the yoke collar on 36in wide fabric without one way

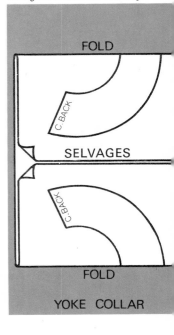

FOLD

C. BACK

SELVAGES

C. BACK

FOLD

YOKE COLLAR

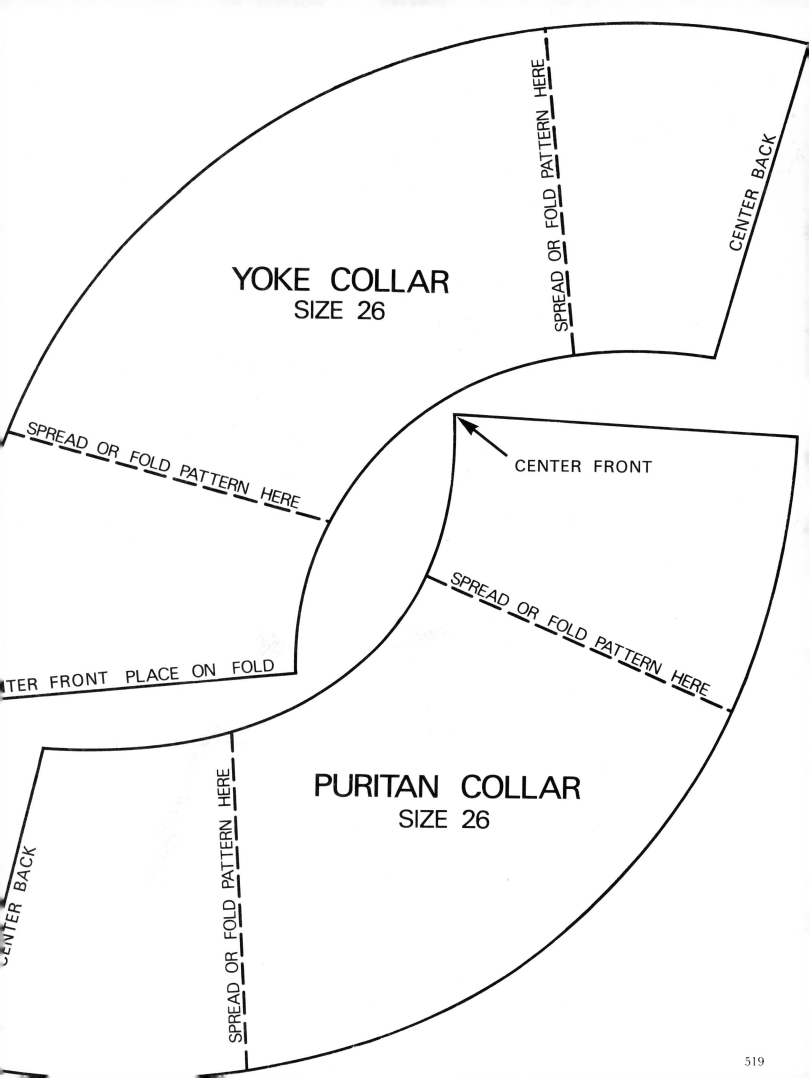

YOKE COLLAR
SIZE 26

SPREAD OR FOLD PATTERN HERE

CENTER BACK

SPREAD OR FOLD PATTERN HERE

CENTER FRONT

SPREAD OR FOLD PATTERN HERE

TER FRONT PLACE ON FOLD

CENTER BACK

SPREAD OR FOLD PATTERN HERE

PURITAN COLLAR
SIZE 26

519

Use the individual motifs for embroidering pretty home furnishings

The tinted areas show two sections given in the following chapters

Furnishing Fashion Flair

Design for a magic carpet

Numdah rugs are traditionally designed with flower and leaf motifs, embroidered with outline stitches in rich colors. In this chapter the corner and part of the border of a typical Numdah design are given, and in the following Furnishing Fashion Flair chapters two sections of the rug center are given, making up the repeats for the whole of the rug pattern.

Each of the motifs in a Numdah design can be used individually and can be adapted for embroidering all kinds of pretty home furnishings. The border illustrated on this page, for example, can be used to edge a tablecloth, either embroidered in an outline stitch entirely, such as chain stitch or stem stitch, or combined with a filling stitch. A bedspread, machine embroidered with the border design, would give a bedroom a glamorous look—or simply embroider the design in thick yarns on loose weave linen for bright draperies. The design will translate into several different techniques —tambour work, needlepoint, shadow work, even rug making—once your imagination begins to work, the possibilities are endless.

Pattern Library

Needlepoint squirrel

This dear little squirrel makes an ideal nursery motif framed as a picture in tent stitch or, worked in cross-stitch, across curtain edges or bedspreads.

The squirrel will measure 6 inches by 6 inches, worked on double-weave canvas, with 10 threads to 1 inch. Work the design in tent stitch with D.M.C. Tapestry yarn in the following shades: 7292 (dark gray); black; 7143 (golden tan); 7176 (terracotta); 7853 (dark marigold); 7771 (bright green); 7911 (deep green); 7745 (pale yellow); ecru which is used for the background.

Squaring up to corners

Where front and hem borders or collars are to be worked for a knitted garment, it is extremely effective to use a mitered corner to obtain a neat look. These edges can be worked separately from the outside edge and sewed on when the garment is completed, or stitches can be picked up for the required length of the border. The illustration of the square neckband, for instance, shows stitches which have been picked up and inverted mitered corners worked to give a neat finish.

As an alternative, by the clever use of a contrasting stitch, a border can be easily worked at the same time as the main fabric of the garment. This method is particularly useful when making square or rectangular shawls and crib blankets.

The child's coat illustrated shows how a contrasting stitch can be used effectively as an edging. The hem and front borders are in seed stitch against a stockinette stitch background. The collar is cleverly shaped inside the seed stitch edge to give a very neat fit and—to continue the theme—the sleeves are edged with a seed stitch cuff.

Seed stitch border

Cast on an odd number of sts, allowing 10 sts for each side border.

1st row. *K1, P1, rep from * to last st, K1.

Rep 1st row 9 times more for lower seed stitch edge.

11th row. (K1, P1) 5 times, K to last 10 sts, (P1, K1) 5 times.

12th row. (K1, P1) 5 times, P to last 10 sts, (P1, K1) 5 times. Rep 11th and 12th rows until work is required length, less 10 rows. Rep 1st row 10 times more for top seed stitch edge. Bind off.

Ribbed edge

Work collar or pocket over an odd number of sts with double-pointed needles for required depth of K1, P1 rib, ending with a right side row. Slip sts on holder. Break off yarn.

1st row. WS is reversed to become RS of work so that first st on needle is P1, use second needle and pick up required number of sts along one side edge, ending with K1 (mark this corner st with colored thread). Work in rib across sts on holder and beg with K1, pick up same number of sts along second side (mark this corner with colored thread).

2nd row. Work in K1, P1 rib to end, keeping corner sts correct.

3rd row. Work in K1, P1 rib to corner st, inc 1 by working into loop between sts, K corner st, inc 1 as before, work in rib to next corner st, inc 1 as before, K corner st, inc 1 as before, rib to end.

Rep 2nd and 3rd rows for required depth, ending with a 3rd row. Bind off in rib.

Garter stitch edge—method 1

Cast on required number of sts and mark corner st with colored thread.

1st row. (right side) K to within 2 sts of corner st, K2 tog, K corner st, K2 tog tbl, K to end.

2nd row. K to corner st, P corner st, K to end.

Rep these 2 rows until edge is required depth. Bind off still decreasing on either side of corner st.

Garter stitch edge—method 2

Cast on as for first garter st edge.

1st row. (right side) K to within 2 sts of corner st, K2 tog, ytf, K corner st, ytf, K2 tog tbl, K to end.

2nd row. K to within 2 sts of corner st, K next st and yo tog, corner st, K yo and next st tog, K to end.

Rep these 2 rows until edge is required depth, ending with a 1st row. Bind off still decreasing on either side of corner st.

Stockinette stitch edge

Cast on required number of sts or pick up sts on wrong side work. Mark corner st with colored thread.

1st row. (right side) K to corner st, inc 1 by knitting into loop between sts, K corner st, inc 1 as before, K to end.

2nd row. P to end.

Rep these 2 rows until edge is required depth, ending with a 1st row. Bind off P-wise.

▲ *Seed stitch border worked with stockinette stitch*
▼ *Rib border worked on collar edges or on a pocket*

Garter stitch border worked from outside edge with simple decreasing at her side to achieve the miter—method 1

Garter stitch border worked from outside edge—method 2
Stockinette stitch border worked from inside

▲ *Stitches picked up and corners mitered for a square neckband*
▼ *Contrasting stitch borders worked on a child's coat*

Sugar'n spice

Light yet warm, this little unlined crocheted coat and matching hat make a charming spring outfit for two-to-three year olds.
The coat skirt is worked in a fabric stitch and the sleeves in single crochet. Use two colors or make it in one—perhaps a pastel or even navy.

Sizes

Directions are for 21in chest. The figures in brackets [] refer to the 22 and 23in sizes respectively.
Length down center back, 13¼ [14:15¼]in, adjustable.
Sleeve seam, 6½[7¼:8½]in, adjustable.

Gauge
9sts and 10 rows to 2in over sc worked on No. F crochet hook.

Materials

Sports Yarn (2oz skeins)
5[5:6] skeins main color A
1 skein contrast B
One No.D (3.00 mm) crochet hook
One No.F (4.00 mm) crochet hook
One No.H (5.00 mm) crochet hook
Three buttons

Back yoke

Using No.F crochet hook and A, ch52[54:56].
1st row Into 2nd ch from hook work 1sc, 1sc into each ch to end. Turn.
2nd row Ch2, 1sc into each sc to end. Turn. 52[54:56]sc including turning ch.
Work 2nd row 2[2:4] times more.

Shape armholes
1st row Ss over 4sts, work 1 sc into each sc to last 4sts. Turn.
Work 1 row. 44[46:48]sc.
3rd row Ss over 2[2:3] sts, work 1sc into each sc to last 2[2:3] sts. Turn.
Work 19[19:21] rows on rem 40[42:42] sts.

Shape shoulders
1st row Ss over 4sts, work 1sc into each of next 11[12:12] sc. Turn.
Complete shoulder on these sts.
2nd row Ss over 2sc, 1sc into each of next 9[10:10]sc. Turn.
3rd row Ss over 3[4:4]sc, 1sc into each sc to end. Turn.
4th row Ch2, 1sc into next 5[6:6]sc. Turn.
5th row Ss over 3sc, 1sc into each sc to end. Turn.
6th row Ch2, 1sc into each of next 2sc. Pull yarn through rem loop and fasten off.
Attach yarn to last 15[16:16] sts and work other shoulder to correspond.

Left front yoke

Using No.F crochet hook and A, ch32[33:34].
1st row Into 2nd ch from hook work 1sc, 1sc into each ch to end. Turn.
2nd row Ch2, 1sc into each sc to end. Turn. 32[33:34]sc including turning ch.
Work 2nd row 2[2:4] times more.

Shape armhole
1st row Ss over 5sts, 1sc into each sc to end. Turn.
Work 1 row.

3rd row Ss over 2[2:3] sts, 1sc into each sc to end. Turn.
Work 16[16:18]rows sc.

Shape neck
1st row Ss over 6sts, 1sc into each sc to end. Turn.
2nd row Ch2, 1sc into each of next 16[17:17]sc. Turn.
3rd row Ss over 2sts, 1sc into each sc. Turn.
4th row Ss over 4sts, 1sc into each of next 9[10:10]sc. Turn.
Work 1 row.
6th row Ss over 3[4:4] sts, 1sc into each of next 3sc. Turn.
Work 1 row.
Pull yarn through rem loop and fasten off.

Right front yoke

Work as given for left front yoke, reversing shapings and working 3 buttonholes, the first on the 3rd row and the third just below center neck edge, as follows:
Ch2, 1sc into each of next 2sc, ch2, skip 2sc, 1sc into each sc to end. Turn.
Work 1sc into each ch on the following row so that the number of sc rem the same.

Coat skirt

Join yoke side seams and shoulder seams.
Using No.F crochet hook and A, join with ss to center front edge of left front yoke.
1st row Ch2, 1sc into each sc along lower edge of left front yoke, back yoke and right front yoke. 115[119:123]sc, including turning ch.
Change to No.H crochet hook and work 1 row sc.
Continue in patt.
1st row Ch1, insert hook between next 2sc 1 row below, yoh and draw a long loop up to level of row being worked, yoh and draw through both loops on hook—called 1 long sc—*1sc into next sc, 1 long sc between 2nd and 3rd sc from previous long sc, rep from * to end, ending with 1sc into last st. Turn.
2nd row Ch1, 1sc into each sc

to end. Turn.
3rd row Ch1, *1 long sc previous patt row, 1sc into next sc, rep from * to end. Turn.
Rep 2nd and 3rd patt rows to form patt.
Continue in patt until skirt measures 6[6½:7½]in from beg, or 2in less than required length, ending with a 2nd row.
Continue in patt, working 2 rows B and 2 rows A alternately until 3 bands of B have been worked, ending with a 3rd patt row. Work 1 row ss with B to finish edge. Break yarn and draw through rem loop and fasten off.

Right sleeve

Using No.F crochet hook and A, ch27[29:31].
Work in sc as given for yoke, inc one st at each end of 3rd row, then every 3rd [4th:4th] row until there are 39[39:43] sts. Work in sc until sleeve measures 4½[5¼:6½]in, or 2in less than required length to underarm.

Shape cap
1st row Ss over 4sts, 1sc into each sc to last 3sc. Turn.
Work 1 row. 32[32:36]sc.
3rd row Ss over 2[2:3]sc, 1sc into each sc to last 2[2:3] sc. Turn.
Work 1 row. 28[28:30]sc.
5th row Ss over 2sc, 1sc into each sc to last 2sc. Turn.
Work 1 row.
Rep last 2 rows 1[1:2] times more. Pull yarn through rem loop and fasten off.

Left sleeve

Work as given for right sleeve reversing cap shaping.

Cuff

Using No.F crochet hook and A, join with ss to first st of lower edge, ch2, work 25[25:27]sc evenly along edge.
Change to No.H crochet hook and work 1 row sc.
Continue in 2 row patt as

given for skirt, beg with B and working until there are 3 bands of B, ending with 3rd patt row. Complete with 1 row ss using B.

Edgings

Using No.F crochet hook and B, beg at lower edge of right front and work 8sc up edge of border, attach A and continue up center front edge, working 38[42:50] sc to neck edge, 3sc into corner st, work 12[12:13]sc to shoulder seam, 13sc along back neck edge and 12[12:13] sc down other front neck, 3sc into corner st and 38[42: 50]sc down left front to beg of border, complete with 8sc in B. Fasten off ends.

Collar

Using No.F crochet hook and A, with RS of work facing, work 33[33:35]sc evenly around neck, beg and ending in 4th sc from center corner sc.
Change to No.H crochet hook and work 2 rows sc, inc 8sts evenly on first row. Change to B and patt as given for skirt, working until 3 bands of B have been worked and ending with a 3rd patt row. Complete with 1 row ss using B. Using B work 8sc along each short edge of collar. Fasten off ends.

Finishing

Press lightly.
Seam sleeves and sew in place. Sew on buttons to correspond to buttonholes.

Hat

Using No.D crochet hook and A, ch5. Join into a circle with ss into first ch.
1st round Ch1 to form first st, work 9sc into circle. Join with ss into first ch.
2nd round Ch2, 1sc into same st, *2sc into next sc, rep from * to end. Join with ss.
3rd round Ch1 to form first st, 2sc into next sc, *1sc into next sc, 2sc into next sc, rep

from * to end. Join with ss.
4th round Ch1, 1sc into each sc. Join with ss. 30 sts.
5th round Ch1, 1sc into next sc, 2sc into next sc, *1sc into next 2sc, 2sc into next sc, rep from * to end. Join with ss. 40sts.
6th and 7th rounds Ch1, 1sc into each sc to end. Join with ss.
8th round Ch1, 1sc into each of next 2sc, 2sc into next sc, *1sc into next 3sc, 2sc into next sc, rep from * to end. Join with ss. 50sts.
9th round Ch1, 1sc into each of next 3sc, 2sc into next sc, *1sc into next 4sc, 2sc into next sc, rep from * to end. Join with ss. 60sts.
10th round Ch1, 1sc into each sc to end. Join with ss.
11th round Ch1, 1sc into each of next 4sc, 2sc into next sc, *1sc into next 5sc, 2sc into next sc, rep from * to end. Join with ss. 70sts.
12th round Ch1, 1sc into each of next 5sc, 2sc into next sc, *1sc into next 6sc, 2sc into next sc, rep from * to end. Join with ss. 80sts.
Work 2 rounds without shaping.
Inc 6 sts evenly on next round. Work 1 round.
Rep last 2 rounds 1[1:2] times more. 92[92:98] sts. Continue in rounds without shaping until work measures 6[6:6½]in from center to edge.
Turn work and crochet brim. Work 1 round, inc 6sts evenly. Work 3 rounds, inc 10sts evenly in each round. Work 1 round without shaping.
Work 2 rounds, dec 10sts evenly in each round. 108 [108:114] sts. Turn work and work 1 round sc. Join with ss. Turn work and with B work 1st patt row. Join with ss. Turn work and with B work 1 round sc. Join with ss. Turn work and with A work 3rd patt row. Join with ss. Turn work and with A work 1 round ss. Join with ss. Break yarn and fasten off ends. Press lightly.

Crocheted coat bordered in pink ►

For those lazy days

Bright and fresh like the countryside in springtime, this attractive afghan and pillow are made out of squares of simple crochet, worked in a clear sharp yellow and three shades of green. Light in weight, they will add comfort and an air of elegance to summer outdoor picnics and later will make warm car accessories for cold, winter journeys.

By using soft pastel colors and omitting the outside round of squares, the afghan pattern could be used to make a warm and practical stroller or crib blanket. Or, matched to a color scheme, the afghan and pillow would add a lively touch to a recreation room or den.

Size

Afghan measures 44in sq.
Pillow measures 9in sq.

Gauge
Each afghan sq measures about 7¼in x 7¼in worked on No.F crochet hook.

Materials

Sports Yarn (2 ounce balls)
10 balls main color A
7 balls contrast B
5 balls contrast C
4 balls contrast D
One No.F (4.00 mm) crochet hook
Pillow form, 10in x 10in

Afghan square

Using No.F crochet hook and A, ch4. Join into a circle with a ss.

1st round Ch3, work 3dc into first ch, work 4dc into each of next 3ch. Join with a ss to top of first 3ch. 16sts.
2nd round Ch3, work 4dc into first dc to form corner, *1dc into each of next 3dc, 4dc into next dc to form corner, rep from * twice more, work 1dc into each of next 2dc. Join with a ss to top of first 3ch.
3rd round Ch3, 1dc into each of next 2dc, 4dc into sp between 2nd and 3rd corner dc, skip 1dc, *1dc into each of next 6dc, 4dc between 2nd and 3rd corner dc, skip 1dc, rep from * ending with 3dc after 4th corner has been worked.
Join with a ss to top of first 3ch. Break off A and attach C in a corner sp between 2nd and 3rd corner dc.
4th round Ch3, 3dc into same sp, *skip 1dc, 1dc into each of next 9dc, 4dc into next corner sp, rep from * ending with 4dc after 4th corner has been worked. Join with a ss to top of first 3ch. Work 2 more rounds with C in this manner inc 3sts on each side of square on every round.
Break off C and attach D as before. Work 3 rounds with D in same manner, inc 3sts on each side of square on every round. Fasten off. Darn in all ends. Work 3 more squares in same manner for center of afghan.
Work 12 more squares in

The color chart shows the sequence of the squares making up the afghan. Each crocheted square is worked using three colors. Put them together by joining the four center squares first.

same manner, using D, C and A in that order. These 12 squares form the 2nd round of the afghan.
Work 20 squares in same manner, using C, A and B in that order. These 20 squares form the 3rd round of the afghan.

Finishing

Press each square under a damp cloth with a warm iron. Join squares on WS using No.F crochet hook and sc. Using D, join 4 center squares. Using A, join 12 squares which form 2nd round, then join to 4 center squares.
Using B, join 20 squares which form 3rd round, then join to 2nd round.
Edging Using No.F crochet hook, work 1 round dc in A, 1 round in D and 1 round in B around all edges, working 4dc into each corner sp on every round. Fasten off. Darn in all ends. Press.

Pillow square

Work as given for afghan square, making a total of 15 rounds in the following color sequence:
3 center rounds in D
3 rounds in C
3 rounds in A
3 rounds in B
1 round in A
1 round in D
1 round in B
Fasten off. Darn in all ends. Work another square in same manner.

Finishing

Press as given for afghan. Using No.F crochet hook and B, join 2 squares on 3 sides with sc. Insert pillow form and overcast 4th side.

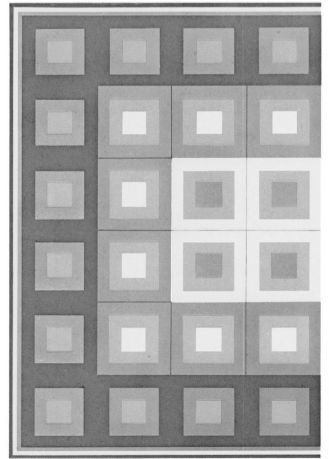

Center

Center

Feel free about embroidery

Embroidery 27

The term "free-motion embroidery" is used when the machine is released from the control of the presser foot and feed teeth so that you can stitch in any direction quite freely. Although designs are usually worked to a pattern, machine embroidery has a degree of spontaneity about it and you will develop a style that is all your own. Be careful not to practice developing a style of your own on one of your favorite garments! Experiment on a scrap of fabric first.

Free-motion embroidery

This is an exciting technique because the designs which can be achieved are infinitely more interesting than those obtained with the foot on the machine or with programmed patterns.

A limited amount of free-motion embroidery is possible on a treadle machine or an ordinary home-type electric machine, but the greatest variety of effects is achieved on swing-needle models.

Embroidery hoops

In free-motion embroidery, the work itself is guided under the needle, the fabric held taut in a hoop. Special machine embroidery hoops which have a screw fitment are available and these hoops are made of either wood or metal. Choose a size suitable for the work—a 4 inch, 6 inch or an 8 inch diameter is used with home machines. Hoops which are only $\frac{1}{4}$ inch to $\frac{1}{2}$ inch deep are desirable.

It is advisable to bind the embroidery hoop with bias strips of material if you are working with very fine or light-colored fabric to prevent your work from becoming snagged or soiled.

Materials

Machine embroidery thread may be available in two thicknesses—No.30 and No.50. Many embroiderers prefer No.30 because it is thicker and less likely to break. Sewing thread can also be used and is available in a much wider variety of colors than the machine embroidery thread.

A No.11 American or No.70 or No.80 Continental size needle is recommended for machine embroidery, but make sure that the needle is sharp. Damaged or bent needles will cause stitches to be missed and make snags in the material.

Refer to Embroidery 26, page 508, before choosing your fabric.

Setting up the machine

First, remove the presser foot and then lower the feed which lies immediately below the presser foot. Some modern machines have a lever for lowering the feed, but if your machine has not got this lever, the feed will have to be covered with a special plate for working free-motion embroidery. The manufacturer of your machine or the local service center will help you to obtain the plate.

These two charming dresses are worked using the free-motion embroider

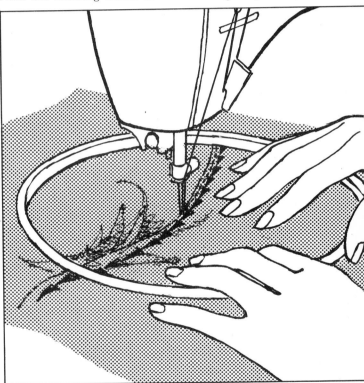

Keep fingers just inside the hoop, well clear of the needle

Thread the machine in the normal way, using machine embroide thread. While you are practicing stitches and effects, use a color thread in the bobbin to contrast with that used on the top of t machine so that tension mistakes can be spotted easily. Tension difficult to check when both threads are the same color.

Both top and bottom stitch tensions should be equal and not t tight—a tight stitch will pucker the fabric. The thread from t bobbin affects the look of the stitch on the top of the work, so lea to adjust the tension screw in the bobbin case. For instance, if t bobbin thread is too loose, the result will be a beady, rough stit on the surface of your embroidery.

To work machine embroidery on a zigzag machine, using t zigzag stitch, set up the machine in exactly the same way, b use the stitch width lever. This will give a much thicker fr embroidery style, either as zigzag or as satin stitch.

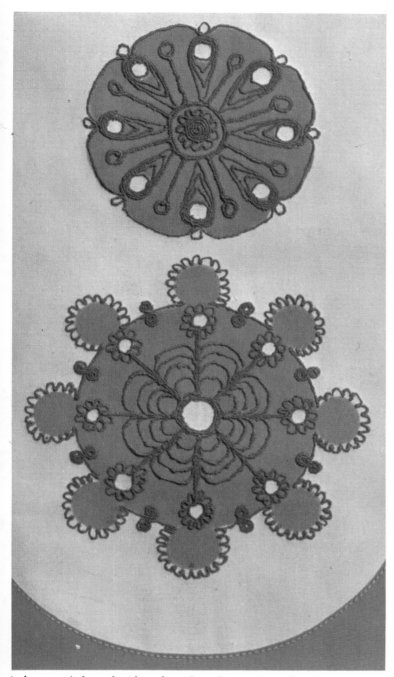

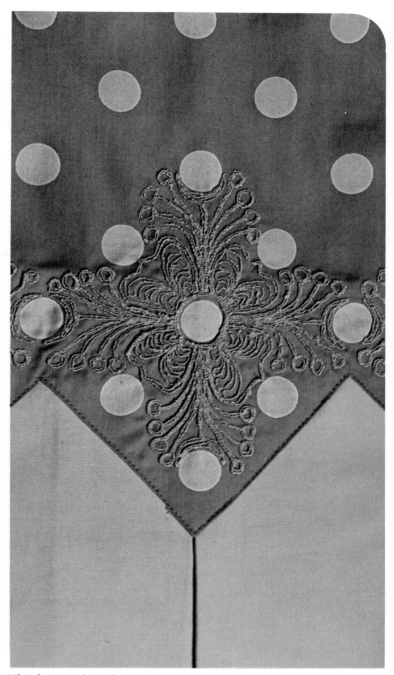

A close-up of the embroidery shows how the use of simple whip stitch (see next Machine Embroidery chapter, page 808) can transform a plain dress

The close-up shows how dots have been used as a base on which to plan a most attractive design to follow the yoke shaping of the dress

Interesting stitches and effects can be achieved by altering tension and by using thicker yarns or metallic yarns. These are explained more fully in the next chapter on machine embroidery.

Preparing the fabric for embroidery

Stretch the fabric to be embroidered tightly across the hoop and then tighten the screw as far as it will go, so that three is no possibility of the material slipping while it is being worked. This is important because without the presser foot on the machine, stitches will be skipped if the fabric is at all slack. Fabric is placed at bottom of hoop—not as for hand embroidery (see diagram).

The method of working

After mounting the fabric in the hoop, place the fabric under the needle and bring the bobbin thread to the top of the work so that both threads are on the surface of the fabric. Lower the lever which would normally lower the foot because this lever also controls the top tension.

Hold both threads in the left hand and start the machine, moving the fabric until two or three stitches have been worked. The threads become locked together and the loose ends can be cut off. You can now move the hoop and fabric under the needle and stitch in every direction quite freely.

Keep the elbows down and hold the hoop with the thumb and little finger of each hand, with the remaining fingers lying just inside the hoop (see diagram). Be very careful not to let the fingers slip under the needle—all too easy to do! Finger protectors, which can be fitted to any make of machine, are available.

After completing the embroidery, remove the hoop, with the threads, very carefully from the machine, remembering that the needle is unprotected.

Rich little rag dolls

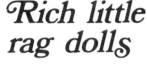

Toy making 3

Introducing two charming little ladies with a delicate air—black-haired Samantha and amber-haired Albertine. The tracing patterns for making the doll's body and a complete set of clothes are given on the next two pages: pantaloons, underskirt, lace-trimmed dress and felt boots. Make one or both dolls for a lucky little girl or for yourself as an ornament for a day-bed or sofa.

Making the basic rag doll

You will need
for one doll 21 inches high

- [ ] Cotton material, beige, white or cream, 28in by 18in
- [ ] Sewing thread to match
- [ ] ½ bag good quality kapok
- [ ] 1oz sports yarn, black or amber
- [ ] Sewing thread to match yarn
- [ ] 6-strand embroidery floss; black, turquoise, pink and orange
- [ ] Fine embroidery needle
- [ ] Felt square 6in by 6in black or brown
- [ ] Sewing thread to match felt
- [ ] Cardboard, 12in by 12in
- [ ] Scissors

Cutting out the body

Trace each part of the pattern onto separate sheets of tracing paper, making two patterns of the legs.

Cut the cotton material in half so that the two pieces measure 14 inches by 18 inches. Place the two pieces of material together, right sides facing, and pin the paper pattern to the material. Cut out the body and leg pieces on the line of the pattern—a ¼ inch seam allowance has been included. Mark the head darts on the wrong side of the fabric with pencil.

Embroidering the features

Mark the features on one of the cut-out body pieces with basting threads. Working on the right side of the fabric, embroider the features as follows:

Eyebrows: in backstitch, using two strands of black floss.

Eye outline: in outline stitch, using two strands of black floss.

Eyelashes: in single feather stitch, using two strands of black.

Pupils: in satin stitch, using two strands of black.

Nostrils and mouth outline: in running stitch, using one strand of black floss.

Eye iris: in satin stitch, using two strands of turquoise floss.

Cheeks: in satin stitch, using two strands of pink floss.

Lower lip: in satin stitch, using two strands of orange floss.

Remove the basting marks after embroidering doll's face.

Making the doll's body

Working on the wrong side, pin, baste and stitch the head, shaping darts on both body pieces. With right sides facing, pin, baste and stitch the two body shapes together ($\frac{1}{4}$ inch seam), leaving the base of the body open for stuffing. Clip into the underarm seam. Turn to the right side.

Stuffing the rag doll

Beginning with the hands and arms, stuff the doll with small pieces of kapok, pushing the kapok in with the eraser end of a pencil. Next, stuff the head, neck and shoulders, leaving the tops of the arms fairly soft, so that the arms hang easily. Finish stuffing the body and close the seam at the bottom of the body. Push the kapok in, using small pieces rather than lumps—otherwise you will not achieve a smooth surface on the doll's body.

Making the legs

Sew the four cut-out leg shapes together in pairs, stitching on the wrong side, leaving the top of the leg open for stuffing. Turn to the right side. Stuff each leg firmly and close the top of the leg seam by overcasting. Sew the legs to the body, placing the leg seams to the front (see diagram).

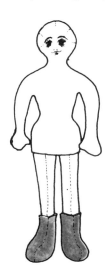

Hair style for Albertine

Cut a piece of cardboard 3 inches by 5 inches. Wind the amber knitting yarn around the 3 inches depth, 50 times.

Slip the yarn off the cardboard, holding it as a skein. Sew the skein to the crown of the doll's head, spreading the yarn so that it covers the back of the head. Sew the yarn to the back of the neck.

Cut four lengths of yarn, 24 inches long. Hold the ends firmly in each hand and twist the yarn. Continue twisting until the yarn coils upon itself. You will find that it suddenly coils and forms what look like three or four ringlets. Pull the "ringlets" into equal lengths and catch them to the head over the ear. Make a similar set of ringlets for the opposite side of the head. Wind some

more amber yarn around the width of the cardboard—this time, 35 turns. Slip the skein off the cardboard and attach the yarn to front of head, covering the top of the ringlets and taking it down to the neck.

Repeat on other side.

Cut off twelve strands of yarn, 12 inches long. Twist the yarn so that it coils up and forms into a bun. Stitch the bun to the top of the head.

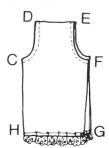

Hair style for Samantha

Cut a piece of cardboard 10 inches wide by 7 inches deep and wind the black yarn around the depth of the card 60 times. Remove the skein and sew it to the crown of the head. Catch some of the underloops of yarn to the back of the neck, leaving remaining loops free.

Making the clothes

For a set of underclothes you will need

☐ $\frac{1}{2}$yd white cotton material, 36in wide
☐ $1\frac{1}{8}$yd eyelet embroidery edging
☐ Narrow elastic

Note: Add $\frac{1}{4}$ inch seam allowance to all clothing pattern pieces.

Making a pair of pantaloons

Trace the pattern of the pantaloons onto tracing paper. Fold the cotton material in half across the width and pin the pattern to the material (leaving enough fabric to cut a strip 24 inches long by 9 inches wide for the underskirt). Cut out the pantaloons (two pieces) and hem along the leg edges. Cut two 12 inch lengths of eyelet embroidery edging and gather them up to fit the hemmed leg edges.

With right sides facing, sew the two pieces of the pantaloons together, joining C to D and E to F; match G to H and sew up inside legs.
Make a $\frac{1}{2}$ inch hem at the waist and insert elastic to fit the doll's waist.

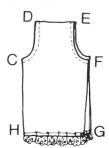

Making the underskirt

Cut a piece of white fabric 24 inches long by 9 inches wide. Make a $\frac{1}{2}$ inch hem along the length of the fabric. Stitch eyelet embroidery edging along the hemmed edge. Make a tuck, 1 inch deep, two inches above the hem. Sew a $\frac{1}{2}$ inch hem at the waist edge and insert elastic to fit the doll's waist.

Making the dress

You will need
- ☐ ½ yard cotton material, plain or patterned
- ☐ Sewing thread to match
- ☐ 3 small snaps
- ☐ 4 yards narrow lace

Copying the design
Cut a strip 36 inches by 12 inches from the material for the skirt. Trace the sleeve, back bodice, front bodice and neckband patterns onto tracing paper. Fold the remaining material and pin the pattern to the material, placing the bodice front on the fold and keeping all the pieces along the straight of the material.

The bodice
On the right side of the bodice front, stitch strips of lace vertically, as shown in the illustration. Join the front bodice and back bodice pieces along the shoulder seams, on the wrong side.

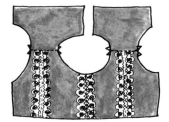

The sleeves
Gather the top of each of the sleeve pieces to take up the fullness so that they fit into the armholes. Hem the edge of the sleeves and attach a band of lace around the cuffs.

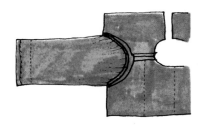

Sew the sleeves into the bodice along the top of the sleeves. Sew the underarm sleeve seam and bodice side seam in one.

The collar
Turn a narrow hem along one long edge of the collar piece. Stitch a length of lace just below the hemmed edge. Right sides facing, place the raw edge of the collar to the raw edge of the dress neckline and sew the collar to the dress.

The skirt
Make a 2 inch hem along one of the long edges of the 36 inch-long piece of fabric already cut. Attach bands of lace, as shown in the illustration. Sew up the side seam, leaving a 2 inch opening at the waist edge. Gather up the waist edge to fit the bodice and stitch the skirt and bodice together.

Finishing the dress
Hem under the back bodice opening and the back skirt opening. Fasten the back opening with snap fasteners, the first at the back of the neck, the second halfway down the back and the third on the waistline.

Making the boots
Using the foot part of the leg pattern up to the "boot line", pin the pattern to the felt and cut out four boot shapes. Stitch the shapes together in pairs, turn right sides out and fit onto the feet. A stitch may be needed to keep the boots on.

532

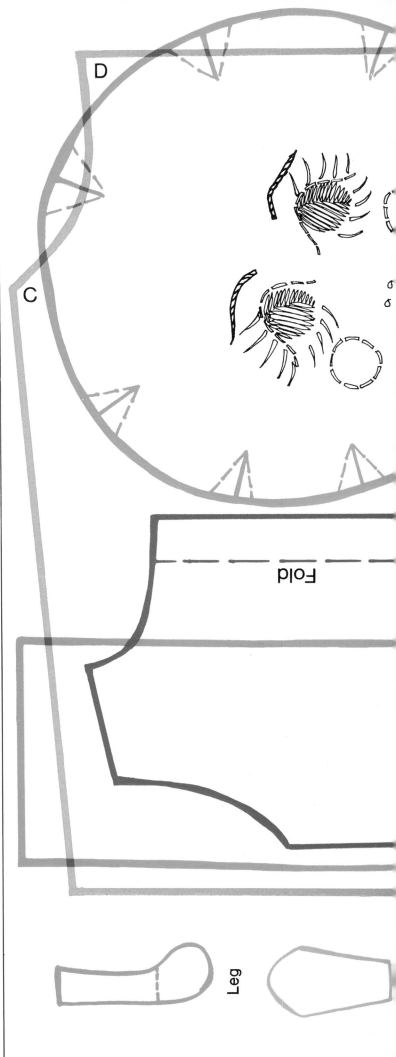

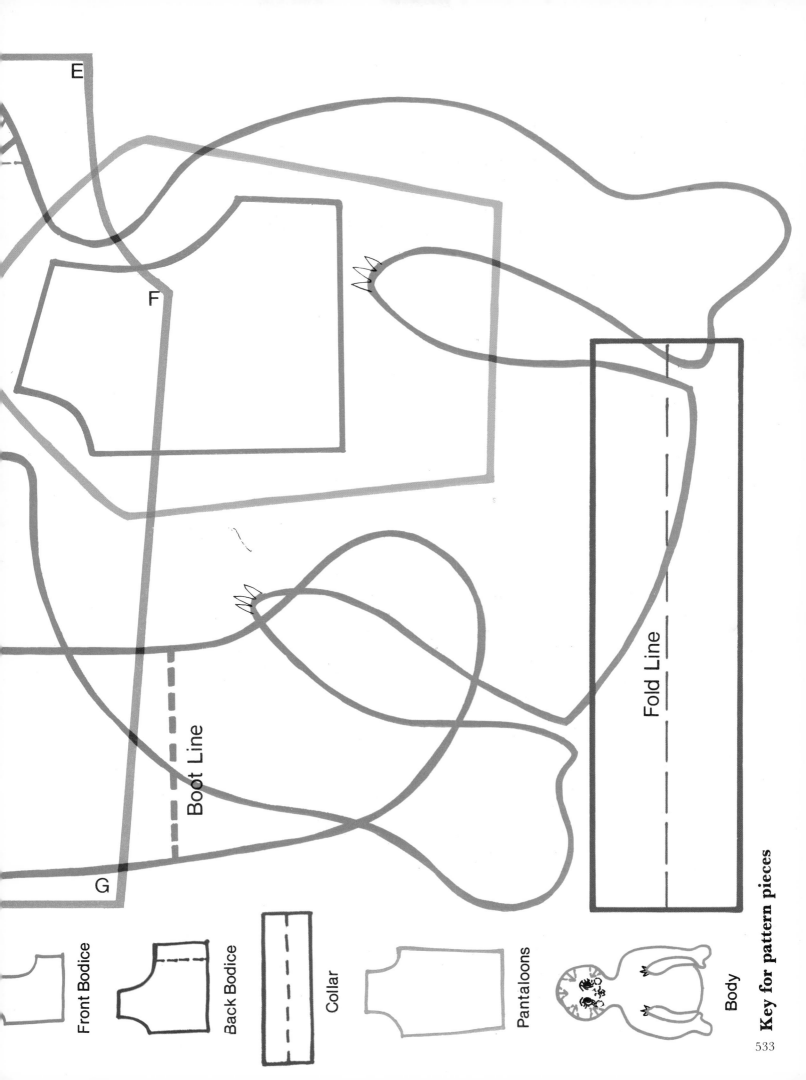

E

F

Fold Line

Boot Line

G

Front Bodice

Back Bodice

Collar

Pantaloons

Body

Key for pattern pieces

533

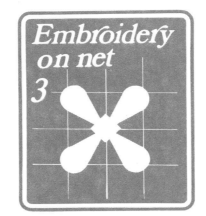

Loopy fillings

The loopy filling below is a simple way of embroidering on net. It can be worked on net curtains or tray cloths, and looks very effective on a delicate net canopy for a crib. You can make it in several different patterns—in double rows to produce a frogged look, in bands of four rows to make a chain of circles, or in thicker bands to cover large areas of net for a really bold effect.

Lacemaking with fishing net

The unusual rustic tray cloth shown on the opposite page worked in soft white embroidery cotton on genuine fishing net.

Materials
You might have to search around if you want to find the rea thing (try ship chandlers or stores selling fishing tackle). Th cloth has been made with $\frac{1}{4}$ inch square netting, and the finishe size is a $9\frac{1}{4}$ inch square. Before the embroidery was worked the netting was dyed russet.

How to do it
Either stretch the net over a square frame with thumbtacks fix it to a thin piece of cardboard with basting stitches. Th will keep the squares even and prevent the embroidery threac from pulling too tightly which would distort the net.
First work the looped filling, starting from the center and workin outward, keeping the loops even and reasonably loose. When th work is completed, remove the frame or cardboard backin and finish off the edges with padded buttonhole stitch. Trim.
Use this edging for the ideas shown in Embroidery on Net chapte 2, page 394.

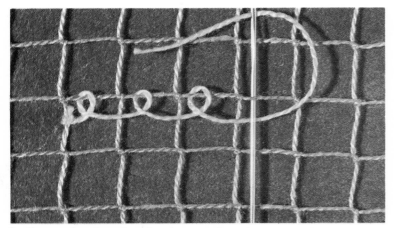

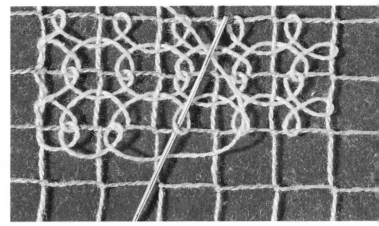

1. Fasten the thread with a knot and work a series of loops across the net over the top bar of each square, carrying the thread over all the vertical bars in between the loops.
2. When you reach the end of a row, loop the thread around the vertical bar of that square and work back again, making a series of loops over the bottom bar of each square. This time take the thread under the vertical bars between loops.

3. Continue working the pattern taking the new loops through those which you have already worked.
4. This illustration shows buttonhole stitch when worked on netting; it forms a striking geometric pattern which can be used very effectively for edging. First, wind one or two threads of yarn along the line of the design and then fasten them firmly to the ne with buttonhole stitch, as shown.

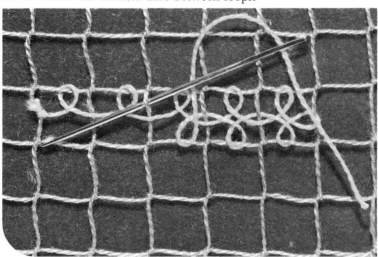

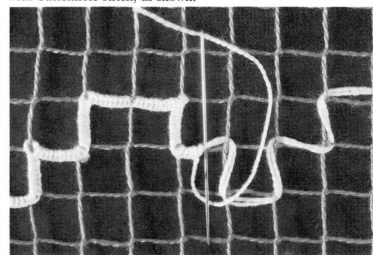

The six-gore skirt

Variations of the basic patterns add versatility and personality to your wardrobe. Making the conversions increases your skill and knowledge of pattern making. In this chapter, the basic skirt pattern is converted to a six-gore, or paneled, version which can be made in three different styles. By adding a slight flare to the panel seams, the skirt takes on a young and lively swing—very flattering for a larger figure. Or, leave the panels straight, and make a beautifully tailored six-gore skirt. The third version with straight panels and a knife pleat on each side of the back panel provides ease of movement, making the skirt suitable for the golf course or the bowling alley. For all versions, use the pattern for the knife-pleated skirt in Dressmaking chapter 15, page 294.

Version 1 — six-gore with flared panels

Extending the pattern
Pin strips of paper 2 inches wide along the panel seam edges on all pattern pieces, as shown in diagram 1.
To make the flare, measure 1 inch out from the point where the hem and side seam meet. Using a yardstick, connect the hipline to this point to make the new panel seamline. Extend the hem to the new seamline.

Suitable fabrics
All the fabrics suggested for the basic skirt in Dressmaking chapter 4 are suitable for the flared six-gore skirt.

Fabric requirements
These yardages are for a 23 inch skirt length.
54in wide fabric, without one way: 1⅜ yards for hip sizes 34½ to 38in; 1½ yards for hip sizes 40 to 44in.
36in wide fabric, without one way: 1¾ yards for hip sizes 34½ to 44in.
One way fabrics: Add about one extra skirt length to all the above yardages.
Extra length: If you want the skirt to be longer (or shorter), add (or subtract) twice the difference in length to (from) the above yardages on both 54in and 36in wide fabric.

Notions
☐ 7 inch skirt zipper
☐ Belt stiffening
☐ Matching thread

Cutting out
Choose the correct layout for your size and fabric width from page 539, and place the pattern pieces on the fabric as indicated. Add ¾ inch seam and 2½ inch hem allowances and cut out the pattern pieces.

536

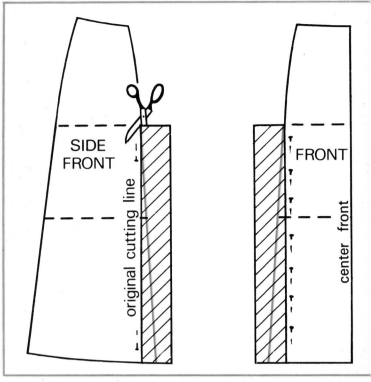

1. ▲ *Extending the panel seams to increase the flare*

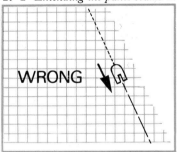
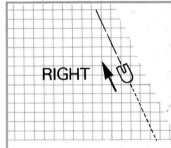

2. ▲ *Stitching into the bias (wrong), and* ▲ *stitching with the bias (righ...*

Stitching the seams on the bias
Because the flare on the skirt has been increased, the seams no... slant toward the bias. This is not a true bias as for the bias-c... skirt, since the seams do not run at a 45° angle to the straig... of the grain (see diagram 2).
It is a good precaution to stitch such seams with the bias, i.e., fro... the hem upward. Stitching into the bias can make the top lay... of fabric stretch, thereby gathering or dragging the under lay... and making the seams hang badly.
Generally, seams should be stitched from the top of a garme... downward, because there is often a little fullness in the fabri... caused by the finish or the weave, which cannot be detected un... the two layers have been firmly joined by machine stitching. If t... seams were stitched upward from the bottom, such fullness wou... be passed into the waistline, neck or armholes, seriously upsetti... the fit of the garment.
Pressing out the fullness before stitching may seem the obvio... answer, but not all fabrics benefit from being pressed first. If t... weave is slightly uneven, the fabric can be distorted. Pressi... before cutting should do no more than remove creases.

Fitting
Baste the side and panel seams. Try on the skirt and follow t... fitting instructions for the basic skirt in Dressmaking 6, pg. 1...

Taking in at the waist. If you need to take in the waist, do not deepen the darts along the panels (i.e., the curved parts of the seams). Leave the panel seams as they are and make one small dart in each side front and side back piece, halfway between panel and side seams. If you take this fullness into the curve of the panel seams at the top, it can create the impression of a big stomach and high seat and the curve becomes too steep to form a good line.

Topstitching the panels

Topstitching the panels gives the seams a little extra support and emphasizes the flare at the hem. You will see from diagram 4 just how effective the topstitched panels look.

If you are topstitching the panel seams they must be prepared. Trim the seam allowances on the front and back panels to $\frac{1}{4}$ inch as shown, but do not trim the seam allowance on the side back and side front sections. Fold the untrimmed allowance over the trimmed one, and baste flat into position.

With the right side of the skirt uppermost, run a row of machine stitches on the panels only, about $\frac{1}{2}$ to $\frac{3}{4}$ inch from the seam. This will look best if you use a slightly heavier machine twist and a larger stitch setting.

3. ▼ *Trimming the panel seams*

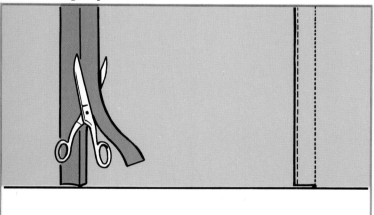

4. ▼ *The topstitched panel seams*

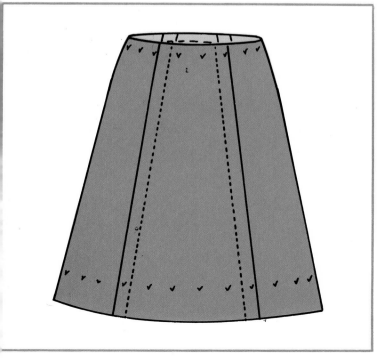

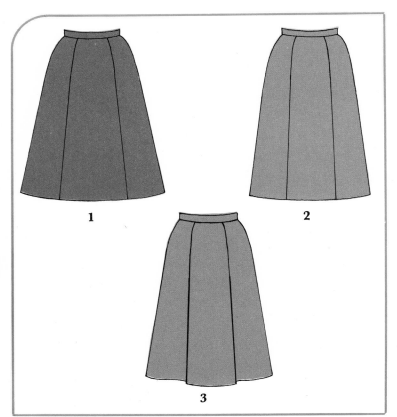

▲ *Three versions of the six-gore skirt:* **1.** *With flared panels.* **2.** *With straight panels.* **3.** *With knife pleats.*

Making the skirt

Apart from the panel seams, the six-gore skirt is made in exactly the same way as the flared skirt in Dressmaking chapters 4-7, pages 76, 96, 116 and 136. You can use any of the waist finishes in chapters 7, page 136 and 8, page 156 ,or insert elastic at the back as in chapter 23, page 454.

Version 2 — six-gore with straight panels

All yardages, layouts and instructions are the same as those for the flared six-gore except that no flare is added to the panel seams; therefore, the instructions for stitching seams running into a bias do not apply.

Version 3 — six-gore with straight panels and knife pleats

Fabric requirements

Calculate the yardage you would need for version 1 as shown, and add an extra ½ yard for the pleats.

Preparing the patterns

To prepare the back and side back pattern pieces for the pleats, add strips of paper along the full length of the back panel seam-lines as shown in diagram 5. The strips should be wide enough to add 2 inches to the seam edges and allow for the curve at the dart. The pleat depth seam edges must be perfectly straight, as shown.

Cutting out

From the six-gore skirt layouts, select the correct layout for your size and fabric width. Using this as a guide, place the pattern pieces on the fabric as indicated, rearranging the pattern spacing to incorporate the larger back and side back pattern pieces. Mark out ¾ inch seam and 2½ inch hem allowances.

Marking the pattern details

Mark all pattern details with tailor's tacks. Then, working on the back and side back sections only, leave the main pattern pieces pinned to the fabric and remove the paper strips from the panel seam edges. Tailor's tack along both panel seam edges to give you the seam-and-pleat lines.

Stitching the pleats

Pin and baste the back panels together along the seam-and-pleat lines and pin and baste the seam allowance on the edge of the pleat depth.
Stitch the seam-and-pleat lines to the point where you want the pleats to open and press the pleat depth toward the center back on each side of the panel. It is advisable to stitch the pleats at least as far as hip level to hold them in place.
Stitch the pleat depth together in the seam allowance from waist to hem (diagram 6).

Completing the skirt

Make the rest of the skirt using the same basic skirt-making techniques and waist finishes as for the flared six-gore version. When finishing the hem, refer to the special finishing notes for the pleated skirt in Dressmaking chapter 15, page 294.

5. ▼ *Extending the panel seams on the back pattern section for pleating*

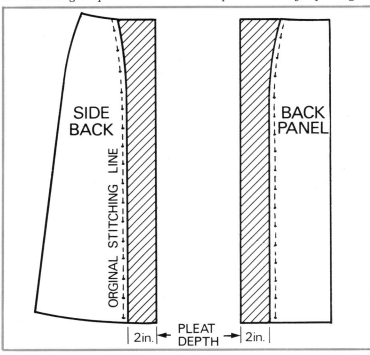

6. ▼ *Side back section showing pleat depth and seam-and-pleat line*

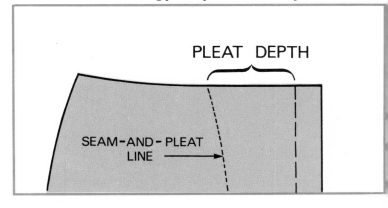

Layout on 36in wide fabric without one way for all hip sizes ($34\frac{1}{2}$ to 44in)

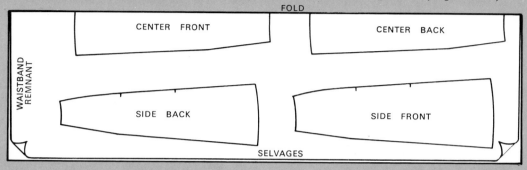

Layout on 54in wide fabric without one way for hip sizes $34\frac{1}{2}$ to 38in

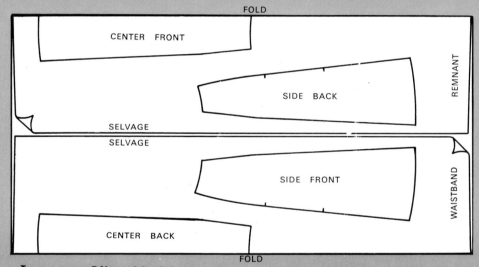

Layout on 54in wide fabric without one way for hip sizes 40 to 44in

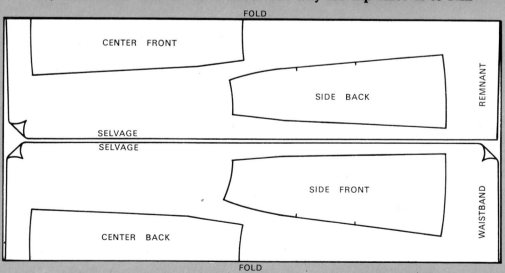

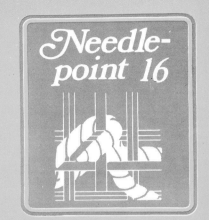

The Red dragon

This dragon design, in a dramatic range of reds and pinks, is shown on a chart so that you can make it in practically any size you wish by choosing a larger or smaller mesh canvas and coarser or finer yarns to correspond (see Needlepoint chapter 13, pg. 458). Work a small dragon to guard your jewels on the lid of a jewel box or a larger one for a wall-hanging. This design would also be impressive on a headboard, pillow cover or rug.

The small dragon is worked completely in 6-strand embroidery floss, while the larger one is worked on heavier canvas using some 6-strand floss together with tapestry yarn and soft embroidery cotton. Using a mixture of yarns will give you experience in variations of texture and show how the planning of different stitches and yarns can add enormously to the finished effect of the work.

Materials you will need

Small dragon (below)

- ☐ Single-weave canvas 12in by 9in with 20 or 22 threads to the in. Finished size measures 7in by 5in.
- ☐ One skein each of D.M.C. 6-strand floss No.352, 351, 350, 349, 321, 894, 891, 309, 326, 603, 600, 605, 3685, 814 and two skeins of 902.
- ☐ Tapestry needle size 22.

Large dragon (right)

- ☐ Single-weave canvas 20in by 18in with 13 threads to the in. Finished size measures 16½in by 11¼in.
- ☐ One skein each of D.M.C. 6-strand floss No. 891, 603, 309, 326, 349; D.M.C. Matte Embroidery cotton No. 2776, 2351, 2570, 2309, 2326, 2304; D.M.C. Tapestry yarn No. 7852, 7850, 7666, 7544, 7208, 7600, 7204; two skeins Matte Embroidery cotton No. 2815, three skeins No. 2572; twelve skeins Tapestry yarn No. 7139.
- ☐ Tapestry needle size 18.

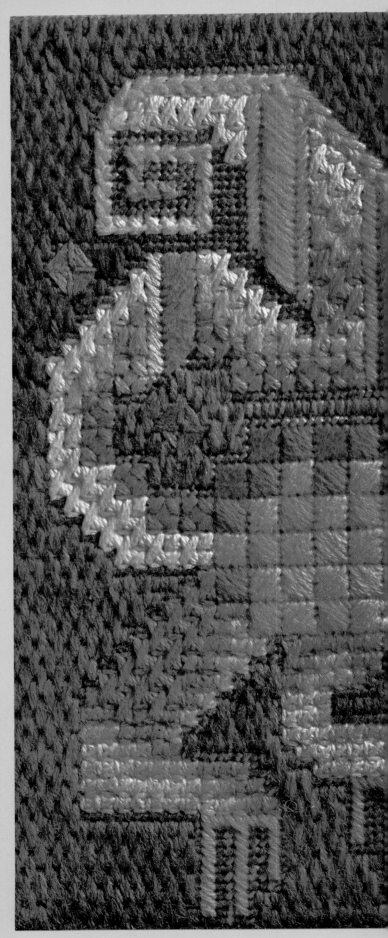

541

How to use the stitch and design charts

For the small dragon, follow the chart using each square as one stitch. For a larger dragon, one square on the chart represents four squares of canvas. The boldly drawn black lines separate different parts of the dragon's body, described on the stitch chart here and small chart, bottom right. The numbers on the stitch chart refer to D.M.C. yarns.

Table (upper)

Part of Dragon	Stitch Reference	Symbol	SMALL DRAGON 6-strand floss	SMALL DRAGON 6-strand floss (12 strands)	LARGE DRAGON Matte embroidery cotton (2 strands)	LARGE DRAGON Tapestry yarn (2 strands)
Tail tip	Long-legged cross-stitch	[symbols]	891 (6), 603, 309		2309, 2572, 2815	
Chest	Alternate diagonal rows of: Algerian eye stitch / Rice stitch	[symbols]	603 (4), 891 (6), 321, 894, 350		2572, 2309 / 2776, 2351	7544
Bands across front legs	Diagonal satin stitch in rows over number of threads indicated by chart	[symbols]	309 (4), 600, 603		2815, 2572	7600
Rest of legs, front and back	Italian cross-stitch	[symbols]	600 (6), 603, 605, 891, 309, 349, 350, 352, 894		2572, 2309, 2815, 2351, 2776	7600, 7204, 7666, 7852
Claws	Padded satin stitch	[symbols]	350 (6), 349, 321, 891, 603, 605	891, 603	2351	7666, 7544, 7204
Hips	Cushion stitch squares, alternating direction. Work backstitch (2 strands) between squares	[symbols]	309 (4), 321, 891, 349, 351, 350		2815, 2309, 2351	7544, 7666, 7850
Flowers	Make a cross as indicated by heavy lines using straight stitches. Work four blocks of satin stitch over arms of cross	[symbols]	326 (6), 309, 350, 891, 894, 603, 600, 321, 814	326	2815, 2351, 2309, 2776, 2572	7600, 7544, 7208
Stalk	Long-legged cross-stitch	[symbol]	326 (6)		2326	
Background	Work 1 row tent stitch around dragon and fill background with alternating tent stitch for small dragon, bricking for large dragon. Use tent stitch between paws and around tail tip. Alternatively speckle by using 1 thread of darker shade with 4 of main		902 (5) / 814 (1)			7139 / 7208

Table (lower)

Part of Dragon	Stitch Reference	Symbol	SMALL DRAGON 6-strand floss	SMALL DRAGON 6-strand floss (12 strands)	LARGE DRAGON Matte embroidery cotton (2 strands)	LARGE DRAGON Tapestry yarn (2 strands)
Eye	Detached eyelet	[symbol]	894 (3 strands)		2776	
Eye surround	1 row long-legged cross-stitch	[symbol]	891 (6)	891		
Nose	Work 1 rice stitch	[symbol]	352 (6)			7852
Upper and lower jaws	Work in cross-stitch	[symbols]	349 (9), 309, 321, 891, 351, 352	349, 309, 891	2815, 2309	7666, 7544, 7850, 7852
Ears	Diagonal satin stitch / Long-legged cross-stitch	[symbols]	600 (4), 3685, 309 (6), 891		2570, 2815, 2309	7600
Mane	In three shades work short bands in padded satin stitch / Work long bands in long-legged cross-stitch	[symbols]	349 (6), 309, 891, 605	349, 309, 891	2351, 2304	7204
Band down back	Work diagonal satin stitch over number of threads indicated by chart	[symbols]	600 (4), 309, 349, 350, 321	309	2815, 2309, 2572	7600, 7666
Top of head and neck	Use upright oblong cross-stitch, filling in odd corners with cross-stitch. Work backstitch (3 strands) between the rows	[symbols]	309 (9), 600, 891, 603, 605		2815, 2309, 2572	7600, 7204
Tail —textured bands	Upright oblong cross-stitch filling corners with cross-stitch	[symbols]	894 (9), 603, 891, 600, 3685	891	2776, 2572	7600
—satin bands	Diagonal satin stitch over number of threads indicated by chart	[symbols]	351 (4), 349, 891, 309, 321	891, 309	2570	7850, 7666, 7544
Blocks at base of tail	Rice stitch	[symbols]	3685 (6), 600		2570	7600

The more threads of canvas worked over for larger eyelets, the more stitches are required for the padded effect. For instance, if each stitch is worked over four threads of canvas, you will need to work over each stitch five times.

upon how many canvas threads are worked over and the number of strands of yarn used in the needle.

The simplest is a plain, square eyelet with eight stitches worked over four threads of single-weave canvas (see diagram).

To make a larger eyelet, work over three or four threads of canvas for each stitch, or alternatively, leave the center

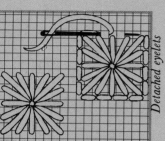

Detached eyelets

around the star until all points are completed (see diagram).

Algerian eye stitch

Work in the same way as star stitch, but work around the star twice, for a thicker, more cushioned effect.

Detached eyelets

Detached eyelets can be worked in different ways, depending

Star stitch

Star stitch is worked in diagonal rows, with eight points in the completed star. Placing the needle through from the back of the work, begin with the top left point of the star. Take the needle through the center hole from the front and then from the back, come through at the second point of the star, to the right. Work clockwise

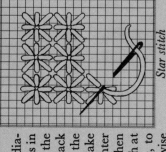

Star stitch

KEY

◤	352
■	351
◎	350
⊠	349
⧄	321
▶	894
·	891

⊙	309
■	326
	902 Background
�￬	603
⊞	600
⊠	605
⬓	3685
◥	814

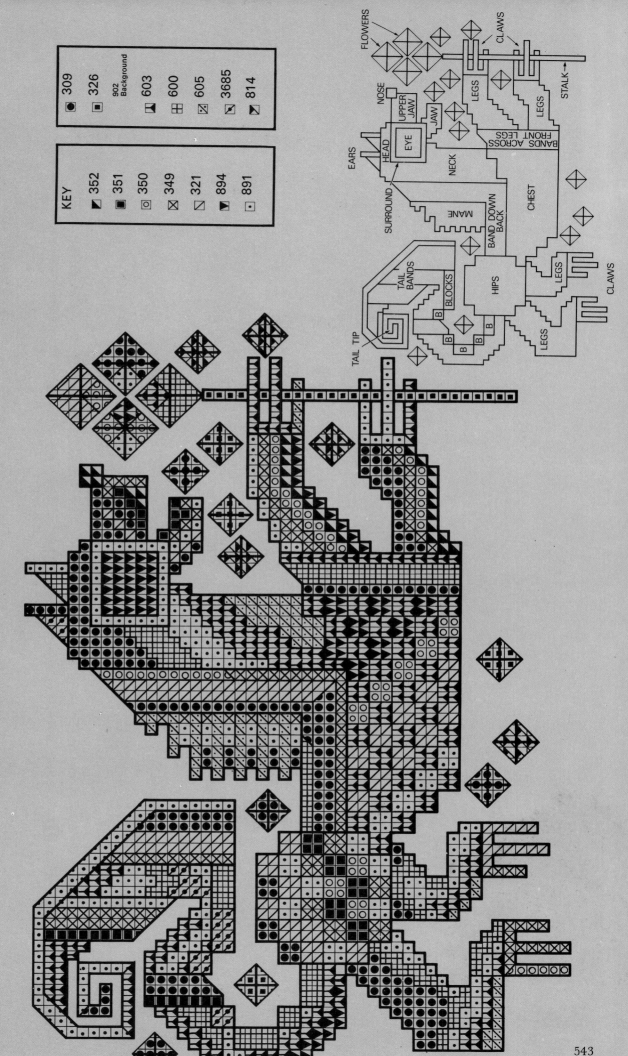

543

Bootee boutique

Take your pick of these delightful baby bootees! The white moccasins, shown on the left, can be worn by both boys and girls, depending on the color of the lace trim. The slipper socks, shown center, are designed for a baby boy while the white lace bootees, shown on the extreme right, would be pretty for a baby girl.

Size
Length of foot, 4in.

Gauge
8sts and 10 rows to 1in over stockinette stitch worked on No.2 needles.

Materials
3-ply Baby yarn
1 ounce main color for each pair
1 ounce contrast color for slipper socks
One pair No. 2 needles (or Canadian No. 11)
Two buttons for slipper socks
¾ yd. ribbon for moccasins and white lace boots.
2 yd. lace for moccasins

Abbreviation
"y2rn" is the abbreviation for yarn twice around needle.

Slipper socks

Starting at upper edge with white, cast on 42sts.
Next row *K1, P1, rep from * to end.
Rep last row 3 times more.
Commence lace patt.
1st row K2, *P1, K4, P1, K2, rep from * to end.
2nd row P2, *K1, P4, K1,

P2, rep from * to end.
3rd row K2, *P1, K2 tog, y2rn, K2 tog tbl, P1, K2, rep from * to end.
4th row P2, *K1, P1, K first loop and then into back of 2nd loop, P1, K1, P2, rep from * to end.
Rep 1st-4th rows 7 times more. Break yarn.
With RS facing slip first 15sts on holder or spare needle.
Attach white to next st and work instep on center 12sts. Work 17 rows keeping patt correct.
Next row K1, P2 tog, K1, P1, P2 tog, P1, K1, P2 tog, K1.
Break yarn.

Work foot
With contrast color, K 15sts from holder, pick up and K 15sts along side of instep, K 9sts from center, pick up and K 15sts along other side of instep, K rem 15sts (69sts).
K 15 rows.

Shape sole
1st row K6, K2 tog, K19, K2 tog, K11, K2 tog, K19, K2 tog, K6.
2nd, 4th, 6th, 8th and 10th rows K.
3rd row K5, K2 tog, K19, K2 tog, K9, K2 tog, K19, K2 tog, K5.
5th row K4, K2 tog, K19, K2 tog, K7, K2 tog, K19, K2 tog, K4.
7th row K3, K2 tog, K19, K2 tog, K5, K2 tog, K19, K2 tog, K3.
9th row K2, K2 tog, K19, K2 tog, K3, K2 tog, K19, K2 tog, K2.
11th row K1, K2 tog, K19,

K2 tog, K1, K2 tog, K19,
K2 tog, K1.
12th row K2 tog, K19,
K3 tog, K19, K2 tog.
Bind off.

Strap

With contrast color, cast on
45sts.
K 2 rows.
3rd row K2, bind off 2sts,
K to end.
4th row K to last 2sts, cast
on 2sts, K2.
K 2 rows. Bind off.

Finishing

Join sole and back seams.
Sew strap to center back.
Sew button on strap end.

Moccasins

Instep
Cast on 11sts.
1st row K.
2nd row K1, *ytf, K2 tog,
rep from * to end.
Rep 2nd row 10 times more.
Break yarn and slip sts
on holder.
Using 2 needle method, cast
on 17sts.
Using same needle on which
there are 17sts, pick up and K
13sts along side of instep,
across center sts K2 tog, K7,
K2 tog, pick up and K 13sts
along other side of
instep, turn and cast on 17sts
(69sts).
1st row K1, *P1, K1, rep
from * to end.
2nd row Sl 1, *K into st
below next st (called K1d),
P1, rep from * to end.
3rd row Sl 1, *P1, K1d,
rep from * to last 2sts,
P1, K1.
Rep 2nd and 3rd rows
5 times more.

Shape sole
Complete as given for slipper
socks. Seam sole and back.

Cuff

With RS facing, pick up and
K 35sts around ankle.
K 3 rows.
Next row K1, *ytf, K2
tog, rep from * to end.

K 6 rows.
Next row K2, (pick up and
K 1, K4) 3 times, K7, (K4,
pick up and K1) 3 times, K2
(41sts).
Commence lace patt.
1st row K1, *ytf, K2 tog,
rep from * to end.
Rep 1st row 8 times more.
Bind off.

Finishing

Sew narrow lace around
cuff and instep.
Run ribbon through
eyelet for ties.

White lace bootees

Cast on 41sts. K 4 rows.
Commence lace patt.
1st row K1, *K1, ytf, K2
tog, rep from * to last st, K1.
2nd row P1, *P1, yrn, P2
tog, rep from * to last st, P1.
Rep 1st and 2nd rows 5 times
more, then 1st row once.
K1 row.

Eyelet row
Next row K5, *ytf, K2
tog, K4, rep from * to end.
K1 row.
Rep 1st and 2nd patt rows
once.

Divide for instep
1st row K16, *K1, ytf, K2
tog, rep from * twice,
K1, turn.
Work 16 rows more in patt
on center 11sts.
Next row P2 tog, P7, P2 tog.
Break yarn.
With RS facing, attach yarn
at beg of instep, pick up and
K 15sts along side of
instep, K 9sts from center
front, pick up and K 15sts
along other side of instep,
K 15sts from needle. K1 row
across all sts (69sts). P1 row.
K1 row.
Rep last 3 rows twice more.
K2 rows.

Shape sole
As given for slipper socks.

Finishing

Sew sole and back seam
and thread ribbon through
eyelet row.

Crochet Know-how 28

Crochet buttoned up

Using the directions given in this chapter, try covering wooden button molds with crochet worked in the same yarn as the garment for an attractive trimming and an exact color match. The corresponding buttonholes can be worked horizontally or vertically as part of the main fabric or as a separate band of crochet, depending on the size of the button chosen and the width of the buttonhole band.

Buttons

Orange button

Worked in sport yarn with a No. E (3.50 mm) crochet hook, this fits a 1½ in. button mold and is suitable for coats and heavy outer garments. Using knitting worsted and a No. D (3.00 mm) crochet hook will produce a button suitable for a cardigan.

Ch4. Join into a circle with ss.

1st round. *Yoh, hook into circle, draw yarn through and pull up into a loop, yoh, hook into circle, draw yarn through and pull up into a loop, yoh, draw through all loops on hook, rep from * 7 times. Join with ss. (8 leaf motifs.)

2nd round. Work 2sc between one leaf and the next and 1sc on the st closing each leaf. Join with ss.

3rd round. Work in sc to end, picking up back loop only of each st and inc 1sc in every 3rd sc. Join with ss.

4th round. 1sc into each sc to end, picking up back loop only of each st. Join with ss.

5th round. Work in sc to end, picking up back loop only of each st and dec 1sc in every 3rd sc. Join with ss.

6th round. Work in sc to end, picking up back loop only of each st and dec 1sc in every other sc. Join with ss.

Fasten off leaving long end of yarn. Thread this end through sts of last round, insert button mold and draw up to fit mold. Fasten off, leaving an end of yarn for attaching button to garment.

Red button

Worked in knitting worsted with a No. E (3.50 mm) crochet hook, this can be used over a 1 in. button mold; however, it is solid enough when stitches of last round are drawn up to act as a button without the insertion of a mold.

Ch4. Join into a circle with ss.

1st round. Work 6sc into circle. Join with ss.

2nd round. *(Yoh, hook into circle not into sc round, draw yarn through loosely) 3 times, yoh, draw through all loops on hook, ch1, rep from * 6 times more. Join with ss. (7 petals made.)

3rd round. Work 1sc into each st closing petals and 1sc into each ch between petals. Join with ss.

4th round. Work in sc to end, dec 1sc in every 3rd sc. Join with ss.

Instructions for making these buttons are matched to the colors ▶

Horizontal buttonholing by chains **2.** *Horizontal buttonhole completed* **3.** *Vertical buttonholing by rows* **4.** *Vertical buttonhole completed*

h round. Work in sc to end, dec 1sc in every other sc. Join with ss. ...sten off, leaving long end of yarn. Thread through tops of ...s in last round, insert button mold if used, draw up and fasten ...f, leaving an end of yarn for attaching button to garment.

...ellow button

...orked in knitting worsted with a No. D' (3.00 mm) crochet ...ok, this can be used to fit a 1¼ in. button mold.
...4. Join into a circle with ss.
...t round. Work 6sc into circle. Join with ss.
...d round. Work 2sc into each sc to end. Join with ss.
...d round. *Yoh, hook into first sc, draw long loop through, yoh, ...ok into same sc, draw long loop through, yoh, draw through ...loops on hook, ch1, rep from * in every st to end. Join with ss. ...2 petals made.)
...h round. Work 1sc into each st closing petals and 1sc into each ...between petals. Join with ss.
...h round. Work in sc to end, dec 1sc in every other sc. Join with ss.
...h round. Work in sc to end, dec 1sc in every other sc. Join with ss.
...sten off, leaving a long end of yarn. Thread through tops of ...of last round, insert button mold, draw up and fasten off, ...ving an end of yarn for attaching button to garment.

...rple button

...orked in knitting worsted with a No. D (3.00 mm) crochet ...ok, this can be used to fit a 1¼ in. button mold.
...4. Join into a circle with ss.
...round. Work 6sc into circle. Join with ss.
...d round. Picking up back loops only, work in sc to end, inc 1sc ...every other sc. Join with ss.
...d round. Picking up back loops only *1dc in sc, ch1, rep from * ...end. Join with ss.
...round. Picking up back loops only, work in sc to end. Join with ss.
...round. Work in sc to end, dec 1sc in every other sc. Join with ss.
...round. Work in sc to end, dec 1sc in every other sc. Join with ss.
...sten off, leaving a long end of yarn. Thread through sts of last ...und, insert button mold, draw up and fasten off, leaving an ...d of yarn for attaching button to garment.

...vo-tone blue button

...orked in knitting worsted with a No.E crochet hook, this can be

used to fit a 1¼in button mold.
Ch4 with first color. Join into a circle with ss.
1st round. Work 6sc into circle. Join with ss.
2nd round. Work in sc to end, inc 1sc in every other sc. Join with ss.
3rd round. *Hook into circle, draw thread through into long loop, yoh, draw through 2 loops on hook, ch1, rep from * 11 times. Join with ss.
4th round. Using 2nd color, work 2sc between each loop st of previous row. Join with ss.
5th round. Work in sc to end, dec 1sc in every 3rd sc. Join with ss.
6th round. Work in sc to end, dec 1sc every other sc. Join with ss.
Fasten off, leaving a long end of yarn. Thread through sts of last round, insert button mold, draw up and fasten off, leaving an end of yarn for attaching button to garment.

Green button

Work as given for two-color button, using one color only.

Buttonholes

Horizontal buttonholes

Work until the position for the buttonhole is reached. When this is worked along with the main part of a cardigan, for example, always finish at the center front edge before working the buttonhole row. On the next row, work a few stitches to where the buttonhole is required, work two or more chain stitches for the size of the button, skip the corresponding number of stitches in the row below (picture 1), then pattern to end of row. On the following row, work in pattern over the chain stitches made in the previous row to complete buttonhole (picture 2).

Vertical buttonholes

Work until the position for the buttonhole is reached. On the next row, work a few stitches to where the buttonhole is required, turn and work back and forth for the required number of rows over these stitches deep enough for the size of button being used, ending at inner edge (picture 3). Work in slip stitch down inner edge of rows to the last complete row worked, work across the remaining stitches for the same number of rows, then continue across all stitches (picture 4).

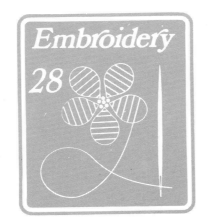

Smocking in fashion

Frills make a charming and feminine decoration for most clothes—smocked frills are even prettier. What was once a decoration solely for children's clothes has now become a fashion note for adults, giving dresses and blouses a new elegance. Add smocking at necklines, cuffs, or in panels down the front of classically styled garments, working and insetting the panels before sewing the garment together.

Decorative smocking stitches

Surface honeycomb stitch
This is worked in the same way as honeycomb stitch (see details in Embroidery 23, p 448) except that the thread lies on the right side of the work all the time instead of being taken through to the back. It is worked from left to right as shown in the illustration below.

Double feather stitch
This is a fairly tight stitch which is worked like ordinary feather stitch, picking up a tube of the fabric for each stitch and working from right to left. This stitch needs a little practice to achieve the even effect required for smocking.

Vandyke stitch
This is a small, tight stitch worked from right to left. Bring the needle through from the back of the work at the second tube from the right. Then work a backstitch over the first two tubes. Go down to the second row, take the needle through the second and third tubes and work a backstitch over them. Go back up to the first row and work as before with the third and fourth tubes. Continue in this way across the width of the work.

The next row is worked similarly, starting on the third row and working up to the second row. Simply thread the needle behind the previously worked backstitches of the second row, as shown. Continue working in the same manner.

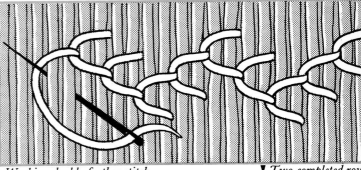
▲ *Working double feather stitch* ▼ *Two completed row*

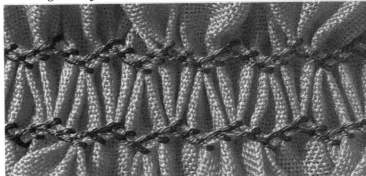

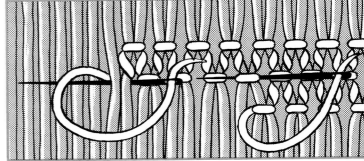
▲ *Working Vandyke stitch* ▼ *Four completed rou*

▼ *Crossed diamond stitch*

▼ *Surface honeycomb stitch*

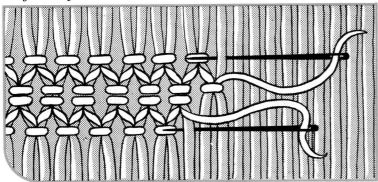

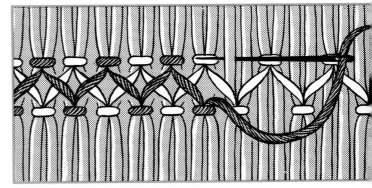

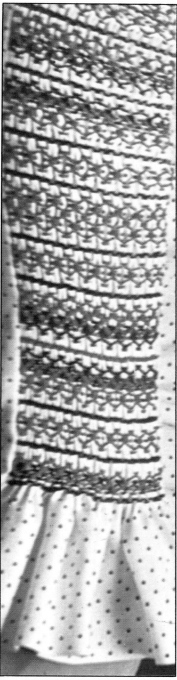

▲ *Detail of inset sleeve panel*

▲ *Inset smocked panels on the sleeves and a smocked neckline make a simple dress pretty*

Putting smocking to work

Smocking stitches are never really complicated and once you have mastered the basic ones it is simply a matter of combining several stitches as in this dotted dress. It may look like an ambitious project, but you will be amazed at how easy it is once you break down the pattern to individual stitches.

This simple dress has been given a touch of glamour by inserting a panel of smocking into the sleeves and adding a smocked collar. You can decorate a handmade dress by inserting a smocked panel, remembering to cut the fabric three times the actual width of the finished panel, plus seam allowances. Once the smocking is completed, stitch the panel in place.

The stitches used on the sleeve from the top downward are:

Crossed diamond stitch: rows 1, 8, 12, 29, 33, 50, 54, 61.
Cable stitch: rows 2, 5, 10, 15, 18, 23, 26, 31, 36, 39, 44, 47, 52, 56, 59, 62.
Diamond stitch: rows 3, 4, 6, 7, 9, 11, 13, 14, 16, 17, 19, 20, 21, 22, 24, 25, 27, 28, 30, 32, 34, 35, 37, 38, 40, 41, 42, 43, 45, 46, 48, 49, 51, 53, 55, 57, 58, 60.

Crossed diamond stitch is worked with two rows of diamond stitch immediately over each other, interlocking one row with the other by working in contrasting colors on alternate sets of tubes (see diagram).

The stitches used on the collar are:
Cable stitch: rows 1, 4, 7.
Crossed diamond stitch: rows 2, 9.
Diamond stitch: rows 3, 5, 6, 8.

Furnishing Fashion Flair

Design for a magic carpet
This pattern is the second section of the Numdah rug design—the border section can be found on page 520. The section of the Numdah design shown here contains two motifs which would work well used on their own or in groups—the daisy motif and the larger flower at the bottom of the pattern, only half of which is shown.

Both motifs can be used as embroidery designs for a wide range of household furnishings—pillow covers, tray cloths, bed linen—or, enlarged, the designs would make an interesting motif for a needlepoint wall panel.